Python 3.14 Fundamentals

Learn Modern Python from the Ground Up

unQbd

Python 3.14 Fundamentals: Learn Modern Python from the Ground Up

Adam Seebeck

For permission requests, contact: https://www.unQbd.com/Contact
PermissionRequest@unQbd.com

Paperback ISBN: 979-8-90377-047-2

unQbd 581 N Park Ave #4201 Apopka, FL 32704 USA

Print Year: 2026

About unQbd

unQbd is a book streaming platform built for modern readers. We publish practical, hands-on books across technical, fiction, and children's categories and make them available to stream from any device for one simple price: $9.99/year.

This book is part of our technical programming series. As a subscriber, you get unlimited access to the full catalog including every title in the series.

Start a free 7-day trial at unqbd.com/app.

About This Book

Python 3.14 Fundamentals teaches the language from first principles using the current CPython release. You will learn syntax, the standard library, and the tools that working engineers use daily, including uv, ruff, pytest, and mypy. The material integrates new 3.14 capabilities, including template strings, deferred annotations, free-threaded mode, and subinterpreters, where they naturally fit rather than treating them as afterthoughts. Every example reflects current best practices and the 3.14 toolchain.

Who this book is for

This book suits three groups: developers writing their first Python code; engineers arriving from C#, JavaScript, Java, or Go who need practical, current Python idioms; and existing Python programmers who want to upgrade their toolchain and code style to the 3.14 baseline. No prior Python experience is required, though familiarity with general programming concepts helps. The explanations map Python patterns to constructs you may recognize from other ecosystems, then clarify where Python differs.

What you will learn and build

You will build a Personal Knowledge Tracker, a CLI application that grows from a single script into a tested, type-checked package. Along the way, you will master values, control flow, functions, collections, classes, and async I/O. You will also adopt professional practices: structured logging, custom exceptions, protocol-based design, and automated testing. Each chapter adds a concrete feature to the tracker while introducing the language or tooling concept that supports it. You will start with a minimal CLI, model data with dictionaries, refactor into classes and protocols, add async metadata fetching, and finish with a locked dependency file and CI-ready commands.

How to use this book (recommended reading path)

The four parts follow a linear path from syntax to production workflow. Part I covers installation, the REPL, and basic script structure. Part II explores the core language through functions, collections, and file I/O. Part III introduces modules, packages, classes, and error handling. Part IV addresses async programming, testing, type checking, and deployment configuration. First-time readers should follow the chapters in order. Experienced developers can skim Parts I and II to reach the 3.14-specific material and toolchain chapters, then study Part IV as a self-contained guide to updating their workflow.

High-level prerequisites

You should understand variables, loops, and functions in at least one programming language. The book assumes no previous Python knowledge. You need a computer running Windows, macOS, or Linux with internet access to install Python 3.14 and uv. All other tools are installed automatically through the project configuration. A text editor and terminal access are sufficient; the book avoids complex IDE setup so you can focus on the language itself.

Table of Contents

Part I: Python Foundations

Chapter 1: Hello, Python 3.14

What You Will Learn

- Install the `uv` toolchain and use it to manage CPython 3.14 interpreters
- Create a new Python project with `uv init` and recognize the generated source layout
- Pin a project to a specific Python interpreter using `.python-version`
- Launch the modern REPL and execute Python statements interactively
- Run a minimal module inside a `uv`-managed environment using `uv run`
- Identify the Personal Knowledge Tracker CLI as the sample application that will evolve throughout this book

Prerequisites

> *No additional prerequisites beyond those listed in About This Book.*

Concept Overview

Python 3.14 is the current general-availability release of CPython, the reference implementation of Python written in C. A reference implementation is the standard version that defines how the language behaves. Most developers run CPython in production.

Two interpreter binaries ship with the release. The standard build is `python3.14`. It retains the Global Interpreter Lock (GIL), a mutex that allows only one thread to execute Python bytecode at a time. The second build is `python3.14t`, an officially supported free-threaded interpreter that removes the GIL. Free-threaded means multiple threads can run Python bytecode truly in parallel. The free-threaded build is opt-in only.

Start with the standard build. Only switch if you have a specific CPU-bound threading workload, meaning tasks that spend most of their time computing rather than waiting for external I/O.

For project management, modern Python relies on `uv`. Astral's `uv` binary replaces `pip`, `pip-tools`, `pipenv`, `poetry`, `pyenv`, and `virtualenv`. It installs interpreters, creates virtual environments, resolves dependencies, and runs commands. This book uses `uv` for every project task.

The Personal Knowledge Tracker CLI is this book's running sample application. It is a local-first command-line tool for capturing, organizing, and searching short knowledge notes. Over the next twelve chapters it will grow from a single file into a tested, typed, async-capable package. In this chapter you will scaffold the project and write its first lines of code.

Step-by-Step Implementation

Step 1: Install uv

Install the `uv` binary using the official installer in your terminal, the command-line interface where you type shell commands.

```
curl -LsSf https://astral.sh/uv/install.sh | sh
```

On Windows, use PowerShell:

```
powershell -ExecutionPolicy ByPass -c "irm
https://astral.sh/uv/install.ps1 | iex"
```

The installer places `uv` in a directory that is typically on your PATH. PATH is an environment variable that tells your shell where to find executable programs. After installation, verify that `uv` is available.

```
uv --version
```

If `uv --version` prints an error instead of a version number, close and reopen your terminal so the shell reloads its environment, or manually add the uv binary directory to your PATH. Once the command succeeds, the toolchain is ready.

Step 2: Install CPython 3.14

uv can download and manage Python interpreters itself. Install CPython 3.14 now; this places the interpreter in uv's managed cache without modifying your system Python.

```
uv python install 3.14
```

Verify the installation by listing available interpreters.

```
uv python list
```

You should see an entry for `3.14.0` or a later patch release. Seeing the version in this list confirms that uv can provision the interpreter on demand.

Step 3: Create the Personal Knowledge Tracker Project

Create a new project directory and initialize it with `uv init`. The command generates a `pyproject.toml`, a `.python-version` pin, and a `src/` tree. If the generated `.python-version` does not already contain `3.14`, overwrite it with the following command.

```
uv init knowledge-tracker
cd knowledge-tracker
echo "3.14" > .python-version
```

The generated `pyproject.toml` looks like this (excerpt):

```
[project]
name = "knowledge-tracker"
version = "0.1.0"
description = "A new Python project."
requires-python = ">=3.14"
```

If `uv init` detected a different default interpreter and produced a lower `requires-python` value, edit the file so it matches the excerpt above. The `.python-version` file contains a single line, `3.14`. Every `uv run` or `uv sync` command in this directory will select the latest patch release of that Python version. Pinning prevents the "works on my machine" problem.

Step 4: Understand the Source Layout

`uv init` creates a source layout by default. A source layout places the package code, the importable Python code for your application, under `src/knowledge_tracker/` rather than at the repository root, the top-level directory of your project. An installed package is what users import after installation. Flat layout, where code lives directly at the project root, is a legacy pattern.

```
knowledge-tracker/
├── .python-version
├── pyproject.toml
├── src/
│   └── knowledge_tracker/
│       └── __init__.py
└── tests/
```

Source layout is the correct default for every new Python project. It prevents accidental imports from the repository root and ensures that test code imports the installed package exactly as users will. Last year I migrated a flat-layout project to `src/` and watched an entire category of CI import failures vanish overnight. Treat flat layout as a legacy pattern. The `uv.lock` lockfile will appear once you add dependencies and run `uv sync`; it is not present yet because the project has no external packages.

Step 5: Add a Minimal Entry Point

You will now add three things: a function that returns text, a function that runs the program, and an execution guard that prevents accidental invocation on import. The `-> str` and `-> None` symbols are type hints; they document that a function returns a string or returns nothing. Python ignores these at runtime, but they help readers and tools understand the code.

Open `src/knowledge_tracker/__init__.py`. Replace its contents with a small greeting function and a `main` entry point.

```
def greet() -> str:
    return "Hello from the Personal Knowledge Tracker."

def main() -> None:
    message = greet()
    print(message)
```

The `greet` function returns a `str`. The `main` function coordinates the program; it calls `greet`, captures the result, and prints it. The `if __name__ == "__main__"` guard ensures `main` runs only when the file is executed directly, not when it is imported as a module. The `-m` flag tells Python to run a module as a script. For `uv run python -m knowledge_tracker` to find an entry point, the package needs a `__main__.py` file that imports and calls `main()`.

Create `src/knowledge_tracker/__main__.py` with the following content.

```
from knowledge_tracker import main

if __name__ == "__main__":
    main()
```

This separation keeps executable behavior in `__main__.py` while leaving `__init__.py` clean for imports.

Step 6: Run the Application

A virtual environment is an isolated Python installation with its own packages. Execute the module through `uv run`. This command selects the interpreter pinned in `.python-version`, creates the virtual environment if it does not yet exist, and runs your code.

```
uv run python -m knowledge_tracker
```

You should see:

```
Hello from the Personal Knowledge Tracker.
```

If you see a `ModuleNotFoundError`, check that you are inside the `knowledge-tracker` directory and that `.python-version` is present. Running the module through `uv` confirms that the source layout is wired correctly and the package is importable.

Step 7: Explore the REPL

Python's interactive REPL is a first-class tool. Launch it with `uv run python`.

```
uv run python
```

At the `>>>` prompt, inspect the running interpreter. The `sys` module provides system-specific parameters and functions.

```
>>> import sys
>>> sys.version_info
sys.version_info(major=3, minor=14, micro=0, releaselevel='final',
serial=0)
>>> sys._is_gil_enabled()
True
```

The `sys.version_info` tuple confirms you are running Python 3.14. The `sys._is_gil_enabled()` function returns `True` because the standard build is active. The REPL supports syntax highlighting and multiline editing. Use it to experiment before committing code to a file.

Exit the REPL with `Ctrl+D` on Linux or macOS, or `Ctrl+Z` followed by `Enter` on Windows.

Full Example

Here is the complete state of the package after the steps above.

`src/knowledge_tracker/__init__.py`:

```
def greet() -> str:
    return "Hello from the Personal Knowledge Tracker."

def main() -> None:
    message = greet()
    print(message)
```

`src/knowledge_tracker/__main__.py`:

```
from knowledge_tracker import main

if __name__ == "__main__":
    main()
```

To run it, ensure your working directory is the project root and execute:

```
uv run python -m knowledge_tracker
```

The project structure should now match the source layout convention:

```
knowledge-tracker/
├── .python-version
├── pyproject.toml
├── src/
│   └── knowledge_tracker/
│       ├── __init__.py
│       └── __main__.py
└── tests/
```

This skeleton is small, but it is the foundation for every chapter that follows. The `greet` function will evolve into note creation logic, and `main` will become the CLI dispatcher. The `src/` tree will expand into `models`, `storage`, `commands`, and `cli` modules. The `uv.lock` file will appear once you add external dependencies and run `uv sync`. Start simple; grow deliberately.

Common Mistakes

- **Mixing system Python with uv-managed interpreters.** Installing Python through `apt`, `brew`, or Windows Store alongside `uv python install` creates confusion about which binary is active. Pick one source per machine; `uv` is the modern default.
- **Forgetting the `.python-version` pin.** Without this file, `uv run` selects a different interpreter on a teammate's machine. Always commit `.python-version` to version control.
- **Adding code at the project root instead of under `src/`.** Files placed next to `pyproject.toml` are not part of the installed package. Keep all application code inside `src/knowledge_tracker/`.
- **Using `pip install` inside a uv project.** `uv` manages its own virtual environment. Use `uv add <package>` to declare dependencies and `uv run` to execute commands. Don't activate virtual environments manually.
- **Omitting the `if __name__ == "__main__"` guard.** Without it, importing the module as a library triggers `main()` immediately. The guard separates executable behavior from importable behavior.

Performance and Production Considerations

`uv` resolves dependencies an order of magnitude faster than `pip`. For local development, this means installing packages in milliseconds rather than seconds. For CI pipelines, it means faster job startup and lower compute costs. Standardize on `uv` for every new project.

The standard `python3.14` build remains the correct choice for production services. The free-threaded `python3.14t` build is available for CPU-bound multithreading. It is somewhat slower per thread than the standard build but can scale work across multiple cores. Do not switch to the free-threaded build unless profiling proves the GIL is your bottleneck.

Source layout prevents import bugs that flat layout encourages. When tests run against an installed package rather than repository root files, they validate the same import paths that production uses. Adopt source layout from day one; retrofitting it later is tedious.

Commit both `pyproject.toml` and `.python-version` to version control. Once `uv` generates a `uv.lock` file, commit it as well. These files are the minimum needed for another developer to reproduce your environment exactly.

Summary

You installed `uv`, used it to install CPython 3.14, and created the Personal Knowledge Tracker project. You pinned the interpreter with `.python-version`, explored the REPL, and ran a minimal module via `uv run`. The source layout convention is now in place.

The Personal Knowledge Tracker CLI will grow from this foundation, gaining new language features, refactors, and tooling in each subsequent chapter. Keep this project directory open; you'll return to it in Chapter 2.

Key Terms

- **CPython**: the reference implementation of Python, written in C. The `python3.14` binary runs this interpreter.
- **uv**: Astral's project management tool. It installs interpreters, creates projects, resolves dependencies, and runs commands in a single binary.

- **Source layout**: the project structure that places package code under `src/<package>/` rather than at the repository root. This prevents accidental local imports and ensures tests exercise the installed package.
- **`.python-version`**: a text file that tells uv which Python interpreter version to use for a project. `uv` reads this file automatically.
- **REPL**: Read-Eval-Print Loop. The interactive Python shell launched with `uv run python` that supports syntax highlighting and multiline editing.
- **GIL**: Global Interpreter Lock. A mutex in CPython that allows only one thread to execute Python bytecode at a time. The standard `python3.14` build retains it.
- **Free-threaded Python**: the `python3.14t` build of CPython that removes the GIL. It is opt-in and officially supported as of 3.14.
- **`if __name__ == "__main__"`**: a module-level guard that executes code only when a file is run directly, not when it is imported.

Mini Quiz

1. **A colleague asks you to add the `httpx` library to the Personal Knowledge Tracker project. Which command is correct?**

   A. `pip install httpx`

   B. `uv init httpx`

   C. `uv run httpx`

   D. `uv add httpx`

2. **The project stores its code under `src/knowledge_tracker/` instead of at the repository root. What is the main benefit of this source layout?**

   A. It allows the code to run without a virtual environment.

   B. It eliminates the need for `__init__.py` files.

   C. It makes the package importable only on Python 3.14.

   D. It prevents accidental imports from the repository root and ensures tests use the installed package.

3. **In `src/knowledge_tracker/__init__.py`, the `main` function is wrapped in `if __name__ == "__main__": main()`. What happens if you remove this guard and import the module from another file?**

   A. The import statement fails with a syntax error.

   B. Python automatically renames `__name__` to `"__main__"`.

   C. The module becomes impossible to test.

   D. `main()` executes immediately during the import.

4. **After profiling, you confirm the GIL is the bottleneck on a CPU-bound multithreading workload. Which interpreter build should you deploy?**

   A. The `python3.14t` free-threaded build

   B. The standard `python3.14` build

   C. The system Python installed by the OS package manager

   D. The REPL interactive shell

5. **A new teammate clones the Personal Knowledge Tracker repository, but `uv run python` selects Python 3.13 instead of 3.14. Which file is most likely missing or incorrect?**

   A. `pyproject.toml`

   B. `uv.lock`

   C. `.python-version`

   D. `src/knowledge_tracker/__init__.py`

6. **You open the REPL and run `import sys; print(sys._is_gil_enabled())`. The output is `True`. What does this indicate?**

   A. The interpreter is running with the Global Interpreter Lock active.

   B. The interpreter is in free-threaded mode.

   C. The project has a syntax error in `pyproject.toml`.

   D. The virtual environment is corrupted.

Answers are provided in the Answer Key at the end of the book.

Activity

- Open your Personal Knowledge Tracker project directory.
- Create a new file at `src/knowledge_tracker/repl_demo.py`.
- Define a function `get_python_version()` that returns the string `"3.14"`.
- Define a `main()` function that calls `get_python_version()`, assigns the result to a variable named `version`, and prints it with `print("Tracker running on Python", version)`.
- Add the `if __name__ == "__main__"` guard so `main()` runs only when the file is executed directly.
- Run the file with `uv run python -m knowledge_tracker.repl_demo` and verify the output.
- Launch the REPL with `uv run python`, then type the following import and call:

```
>>> from knowledge_tracker.repl_demo import get_python_version
>>> get_python_version()
'3.14'
```

- You'll confirm that importing the module does not trigger the print statement from `main()`.

Chapter 2: Values, Expressions, Strings, and Types

What You Will Learn

- Create and manipulate Python's core built-in values: numbers, strings, booleans, and None
- Format output with f-strings and format specifications for readable CLI previews
- Construct Python 3.14 template strings and explain why they differ from f-strings
- Model lightweight domain data using dictionaries for the Personal Knowledge Tracker CLI
- Annotate variables and functions with type hints while respecting Python's dynamic nature
- Inspect types at runtime with `type()` and `isinstance()`

Prerequisites

- Completion of Chapter 1
- Ability to create a project with `uv init` and run code with `uv run python`
- Familiarity with the `greet` and `main` entry points in the Personal Knowledge Tracker CLI

Concept Overview

Everything in Python is an object. Numbers, strings, functions, and even types themselves live on the heap and are referenced by names. This object model shapes how Python handles assignment, argument passing, and memory management. Unlike C# or Java, Python doesn't declare variables with fixed types; names are bound to objects dynamically, and the type checker is an external tool, not the interpreter.

Strings are first-class citizens in a CLI application. The Personal Knowledge Tracker renders note titles, tags, and previews to the terminal. Python offers several ways to build strings: concatenation, the `str.format` method, f-strings, and (new in 3.14) template strings. F-strings are the default choice for readable formatting. Template strings, created with the `t"..."` prefix, return a `string.templatelib.Template` object that separates the template structure from its rendering. This separation makes context-aware escaping possible, which matters when you export notes to HTML or inject values into structured formats.

Use f-strings for CLI output. Reserve t-strings for escaping pipelines.

For data modeling, dictionaries provide a lightweight way to group related fields. A note in the tracker starts as a dictionary with keys for title, body, tags, creation time, and an optional source URL. Dictionaries are flexible, but flexibility can hide errors. Type hints and PEP 695 type aliases document the expected shape of these dictionaries without changing runtime behavior.

Step-by-Step Implementation

Step 1: Values and Numeric Types

Open `src/knowledge_tracker/ch02_values.py` in your editor. Python integers (`int`) have arbitrary precision, while floating-point numbers (`float`) are IEEE 754 double-precision values. Both support the usual arithmetic operators.

```
note_count: int = 42
pi_approx: float = 3.14159
total: float = note_count + pi_approx

print(type(note_count))
print(type(total))
print(total)
```

Running this with `uv run python src/knowledge_tracker/ch02_values.py` prints `<class 'int'>`, `<class 'float'>`, and `45.14159`. The name `note_count` refers to an `int` object. The name `total` refers to a new `float` object produced by the addition. Python coerced the result to `float` automatically because one operand was a float.

Types are determined at runtime.

Names are not boxes that hold values; they are references to objects. Assignment never copies data; it binds a name to an object. This distinction becomes critical when you pass mutable collections to functions in later chapters.

Booleans and `None` are distinct built-in types. `True` and `False` are the only `bool` instances, while `None` is a singleton representing the absence of a value. Always compare to `None` with `is` or `is not`.

```
is_active: bool = True
pending: str | None = None

print(is_active, pending is None)
print(bool(0), bool(""), bool(42), bool("hello"))
```

Truthiness means that `0`, empty strings, and `None` evaluate to `False` in a conditional. Non-zero numbers and non-empty strings evaluate to `True`. Use `is None` rather than `== None` to avoid triggering custom equality logic.

Step 2: String Operations and Formatting

Strings are immutable sequences of Unicode code points. Slicing returns a new string; the original is unchanged.

Slice boundaries are exclusive.

For the tracker, add two helpers: one that truncates long titles for compact previews, and one that formats tag lists.

```
def truncate_title(title: str, width: int = 40) -> str:
    if len(title) <= width:
        return title
    if width < 3:
        return title[:width]
    return title[:width - 3] + "..."

def format_tags(tags: list[str]) -> str:
    if not tags:
        return "no tags"
    return ", ".join(f"#{tag}" for tag in tags)
```

`truncate_title` now honors `width` exactly. If the title fits, it returns the original. If `width` is smaller than the ellipsis length, it returns a raw slice. `format_tags` uses a generator expression inside `join` to lazily format each tag with a `#` prefix. The generator yields one formatted tag at a time without building an intermediate list.

Format specifications control how values are rendered inside f-strings.

```
print(f"Pi is roughly {pi_approx:.2f}")
```

The `:.2f` inside the braces rounds the float to two decimal places. In an f-string the format spec is applied immediately and the result is eagerly turned into a `str`. A template string does not apply the format spec automatically; it captures the spec as the `.format_spec` field on each `Interpolation` and produces no `str` until a consumer renders the template and chooses whether to apply it.

Step 3: Template Strings

Python 3.14 introduces template strings with the `t"..."` prefix. A template string does not produce a `str`. It produces a `string.templatelib.Template` whose `.strings` and `.interpolations` attributes let the caller control rendering.

You can inspect a template before rendering by iterating over it. Each item is either a `str` or an `Interpolation`.

Add a safe HTML renderer that escapes dynamic values.

```
from html import escape
from string.templatelib import Interpolation, Template

def render_safe_html(template: Template) -> str:
    parts: list[str] = []
    for item in template:
        if isinstance(item, str):
            parts.append(item)
        elif isinstance(item, Interpolation):
            parts.append(escape(str(item.value)))
    return "".join(parts)
```

The `for` loop iterates over the template. Each `Interpolation` exposes `.value` (the evaluated object), `.expression` (the source text), `.conversion`, and

`.format_spec`. By intercepting the value before it becomes a string, the renderer can apply context-aware escaping. An f-string would have already rendered the raw value into the output, leaving no hook for escaping.

Demonstrate the difference:

```
user_input = "<script>alert('xss')</script>"
template = t"<p>Note: {user_input}</p>"

print(render_safe_html(template))
```

The output escapes the script tag. If you had used an f-string, the raw HTML would have been emitted immediately. Use template strings when you need to inspect or sanitize interpolations before rendering.

Step 4: Dynamic Typing and Type Aliases

Python checks types while the program runs, not before. A name can refer to an integer in one moment and a string in the next. Type hints are annotations that tools like mypy read; the interpreter ignores them.

Add a type alias for the tracker's note dictionaries using PEP 695 syntax, and a small inspection helper.

```
type NoteDict = dict[str, str | list[str] | None]
```

The `|` operator in a type hint means union; the value may be any of the listed types. `NoteDict` describes a dictionary whose keys are strings and whose values may be strings, lists of strings, or `None`. The `X | Y` union operator requires Python 3.10 or later, while the `type` alias statement shown here is PEP 695 syntax that requires Python 3.12 or later.

Annotations have no runtime effect.

The `object` annotation on `inspect_value` accepts any value because every Python type inherits from `object`. Inside the f-string, the `!r` conversion calls `repr()` and produces a developer-friendly string that preserves type information.

```
def inspect_value(value: object) -> str:
    return f"Type: {type(value).__name__}, Value: {value!r}"
```

You can verify types at runtime when necessary:

```
sample: object = 3.14
print(inspect_value(sample))
print(isinstance(sample, float))
```

`isinstance` is preferred over `type(x) is SomeType` because it respects inheritance.

Don't use `type() is` for runtime checks. Prefer `isinstance` always.

Resist the urge to scatter `isinstance` checks everywhere; they clutter functions and fight the grain of duck typing.

Step 5: Note Modeling with Dictionaries

Dictionaries map keys to values and provide O(1) average-time lookups. They are the right tool for prototyping the tracker's data model before we introduce dataclasses in Chapter 8.

Add a factory function that creates a note dictionary.

```
from datetime import datetime, timezone

def create_note(
    title: str,
    body: str,
    tags: list[str],
    source_url: str | None = None,
) -> NoteDict:
    return {
        "title": title,
        "body": body,
        "tags": tags,
        "created": datetime.now(timezone.utc).isoformat(),
        "source_url": source_url,
    }
```

`create_note` returns a `NoteDict` with an ISO 8601 timestamp. The dictionary literal groups related fields into a single value. The `source_url` parameter defaults to `None`, so callers can omit it.

Next, add a preview function that consumes the dictionary.

```
def preview_note(note: NoteDict) -> str:
    title = truncate_title(str(note.get("title", "")))
    raw_tags = note.get("tags")
    tag_list: list[str] = raw_tags if isinstance(raw_tags, list) else
[]
    tags = format_tags(tag_list)
    return f"{title} [{tags}]"
```

`preview_note` uses `.get()` to avoid `KeyError` when a key is missing. It validates that `tags` is a list before passing it to `format_tags`. Malformed data won't crash the CLI during early development.

A missing dictionary key once crashed a production CLI I maintained.

Step 6: Bringing It Together

Recreate the Chapter 1 entry points so the module remains runnable without cross-file imports.

```
import sys

def greet() -> str:
    return "Hello from the Personal Knowledge Tracker."

def get_python_version() -> int:
    return sys.version_info.major
```

Then add a demonstration function that exercises the code from the previous steps.

```
def demo_notes() -> None:
    print(get_python_version())
    print(greet())

    note = create_note(
        title="Python 3.14 Template Strings",
        body="Template strings separate structure from rendering.",
        tags=["python", "strings"],
        source_url="https://docs.python.org/3.14/whatsnew/3.14.html",
    )

    print(preview_note(note))
    print(inspect_value(note))

    user_input = "<script>alert('xss')</script>"
    template = t"<p>Note: {user_input}</p>"
    print(render_safe_html(template))
```

```
if __name__ == "__main__":
    demo_notes()
```

Full Example

The following script consolidates every helper, type alias, and function introduced in the step-by-step. It also recreates the Chapter 1 entry points so the file is fully self-contained. Save this as `src/knowledge_tracker/ch02_values.py` and run it with `uv run python src/knowledge_tracker/ch02_values.py`.

```
import sys
from datetime import datetime, timezone
from html import escape
from string.templatelib import Interpolation, Template

def greet() -> str:
    return "Hello from the Personal Knowledge Tracker."

def get_python_version() -> int:
    return sys.version_info.major

def truncate_title(title: str, width: int = 40) -> str:
    if len(title) <= width:
        return title
    if width < 3:
        return title[:width]
    return title[:width - 3] + "..."

def format_tags(tags: list[str]) -> str:
    if not tags:
        return "no tags"
    return ", ".join(f"#{tag}" for tag in tags)

def render_safe_html(template: Template) -> str:
    parts: list[str] = []
    for item in template:
        if isinstance(item, str):
            parts.append(item)
        elif isinstance(item, Interpolation):
            parts.append(escape(str(item.value)))
    return "".join(parts)

type NoteDict = dict[str, str | list[str] | None]

def inspect_value(value: object) -> str:
    return f"Type: {type(value).__name__}, Value: {value!r}"
```

```
def create_note(
    title: str,
    body: str,
    tags: list[str],
    source_url: str | None = None,
) -> NoteDict:
    return {
        "title": title,
        "body": body,
        "tags": tags,
        "created": datetime.now(timezone.utc).isoformat(),
        "source_url": source_url,
    }

def preview_note(note: NoteDict) -> str:
    title = truncate_title(str(note.get("title", "")))
    raw_tags = note.get("tags")
    tag_list: list[str] = raw_tags if isinstance(raw_tags, list) else
[]
    tags = format_tags(tag_list)
    return f"{title} [{tags}]"

def demo_notes() -> None:
    print(get_python_version())
    print(greet())

    note = create_note(
        title="Python 3.14 Template Strings",
        body="Template strings separate structure from rendering.",
        tags=["python", "strings"],
        source_url="https://docs.python.org/3.14/whatsnew/3.14.html",
    )

    print(preview_note(note))
    print(inspect_value(note))

    user_input = "<script>alert('xss')</script>"
    template = t"<p>Note: {user_input}</p>"
    print(render_safe_html(template))

if __name__ == "__main__":
    demo_notes()
```

This module is intentionally self-contained. `truncate_title` and `format_tags` handle presentation concerns. `render_safe_html` shows how 3.14 template strings enable safe rendering pipelines. `create_note` and `preview_note` establish the dictionary-based model for the Personal Knowledge Tracker CLI that will persist to disk in Chapter 6 and evolve into a dataclass in Chapter 8.

Common Mistakes

- **Confusing template strings with f-strings.** A `t"..."` literal returns a `Template` object, not a `str`. Passing it to a function that expects a string will raise `TypeError`. Use `t"..."` only when you need to intercept interpolations; otherwise use f-strings.
- **Expecting type hints to enforce behavior at runtime.** Python ignores annotations. A variable annotated as `int` can still hold a string. Use mypy or pyright to catch type errors before execution.
- **Using `type(x) is SomeType` instead of `isinstance(x, SomeType)`.** The `is` check ignores inheritance and breaks with subclasses. Always prefer `isinstance` for runtime type checks.
- **Mutating a string in place.** Strings are immutable. Methods like `upper()` or slices like `s[:5]` return new objects. Assign the result back to a name if you need to keep it.
- **Accessing dictionary keys directly without checking existence.** `note["title"]` raises `KeyError` if the key is missing. Use `.get()` with a default when the data shape is uncertain.
- **Forgetting that `None` is a singleton.** Compare to `None` with `is` or `is not`, not ==. While == often works, `is` communicates intent clearly and avoids overridden `__eq__` behavior.

Performance and Production Considerations

- **F-strings are the fastest formatting option for simple cases.** They are parsed at compile time and evaluated with minimal overhead. Use them for logs and CLI output unless you need the structural separation that template strings provide.
- **Template strings allocate more objects than f-strings.** Each `t"..."` produces a `Template` containing `Interpolation` instances. Do not use them in tight loops where raw f-strings suffice. Reserve template strings for rendering pipelines that require escaping or internationalization.
- **Dictionary access is fast, but key errors are not.** A failed key lookup raises an exception that unwinds the stack. Use `.get()` for

optional fields, and validate external data before inserting it into a dictionary that downstream code treats as well-formed.

- **`isinstance` checks in hot paths add overhead.** Runtime type inspection is slower than direct attribute access. Keep type hints static; do not use `isinstance` as a substitute for proper API design.
- **Immutable strings simplify concurrency.** Because strings cannot change after creation, they are safe to share across threads without locks. This property becomes relevant in Chapter 10 when the tracker fetches URL metadata concurrently.

Summary

Python represents all data as objects referenced by names. Numeric types support the usual arithmetic, strings provide flexible slicing and formatting tools, and dictionaries group related fields into a single value. F-strings remain the standard for readable string formatting, while Python 3.14 template strings introduce a structural layer that enables safe, context-aware rendering. Type hints and PEP 695 aliases document intent for developers and static analyzers without altering the dynamic behavior of the interpreter. The Personal Knowledge Tracker CLI now has a lightweight dictionary-based model for notes, string helpers for previews, and a foundation that will carry forward as the project grows.

Key Terms

- **Object**: Every value in Python is an object; names are references to objects, not containers of data.
- **F-string**: A formatted string literal using the `f"..."` prefix that evaluates embedded expressions at runtime.
- **Template string**: A literal using the `t"..."` prefix that returns a `string.templatelib.Template`, separating structure from rendering.
- **Type hint**: An annotation indicating the expected type of a name; read by static analyzers but ignored by the interpreter.
- **Type alias**: A named shorthand for a complex type declared with `type Name = ...` (PEP 695).

- **Dynamic typing**: The runtime behavior where names can bind to objects of any type and type errors surface during execution.
- **Dictionary**: A mutable mapping of keys to values; the tracker uses dictionaries to prototype note data.
- **None**: The singleton representing the absence of a value; compare it using `is` or `is not`.

Mini Quiz

1. **What is the output of the following code?**

```
count: int = "five"
print(type(count))
```

   A. `<class 'int'>`

   B. `<class 'object'>`

   C. `TypeError`

   D. `<class 'str'>`

2. **A legacy import in the Personal Knowledge Tracker produces note dictionaries that may lack the `"tags"` key. Which access pattern prevents a `KeyError` when reading tags?**

   A. `note.get("tags", [])`

   B. `note["tags"]`

   C. `note.tags`

   D. `note["tags"] or []`

3. **In Python 3.14, what is the primary advantage of a template string (`t"..."`) over an f-string (`f"..."`)?**

   A. Template strings compile faster and use less memory.

   B. Template strings automatically escape HTML and SQL injection attempts.

   C. Template strings expose the static and dynamic parts so callers can control rendering.

   D. Template strings return a plain `str` that requires no further processing.

4. **Which statement about the PEP 695 type alias `type NoteDict = dict[str, str | list[str] | None]` is correct?**

   A. It creates a runtime validator that rejects malformed dictionaries.

   B. It defines a new dictionary subclass called `NoteDict`.

   C. It serves as documentation for developers and static type checkers.

   D. It is only valid inside a class definition.

5. **Why is `isinstance(value, float)` preferred over `type(value) is float`?**

   A. `isinstance` executes faster in tight loops.

   B. `isinstance` can check an unlimited number of types without a tuple.

   C. `type()` is deprecated in Python 3.14.

   D. `isinstance` respects inheritance and accepts subclasses of `float`.

Answers are provided in the Answer Key at the end of the book.

Activity

- Create a new file named `ch02_activity.py` in your project directory.
- Copy the `NoteDict` type alias, `format_tags`, and `render_safe_html` definitions from `ch02_values.py` into the new module. If you don't have a `create_note` helper from the chapter code, build sample dictionaries directly: `{"title": "...", "body": "...", "tags": ["python"], "created": "2025-01-01T00:00:00", "source_url": None}`.
- Define a function `find_notes_by_tag(notes: list[NoteDict], tag: str) -> list[NoteDict]` that iterates over the list and returns only notes where the `"tags"` key exists, is a list, and contains the requested tag. Don't assume the key exists; use `.get()` and `isinstance` for safety.
- Define a function `export_note_plaintext(note: NoteDict) -> str` that returns a formatted string containing the note title, creation time, tags, and body. Use an f-string and reuse `format_tags`.
- Define a function `note_to_html(note: NoteDict) -> str` that builds a template string from the note title and body, then returns the result of `render_safe_html`.
- Write a `demo()` function that creates three note dictionaries with different tags, searches for the tag `"python"`, and prints the plaintext export and HTML output of the first match.
- Run the script with `uv run python ch02_activity.py`. Confirm that any HTML characters in the note body are escaped in the HTML output but remain literal in the plaintext export.

Chapter 3: Control Flow and CLI Routing

What You Will Learn

- Evaluate conditions using Python truthiness and membership tests
- Branch execution with `if`, `elif`, and `else`
- Iterate with `for` and `while`, including `break`, `continue`, and loop `else`
- Route behavior with `match` and `case` structural pattern matching
- Parse CLI arguments using `argparse` subparsers
- Build a runnable Personal Knowledge Tracker CLI that creates, lists, and searches notes in memory
- Understand that the in-memory note store is process-local and ephemeral until persistence is introduced in Chapter 6

Prerequisites

- Completion of Chapter 1 (project setup with `uv`, source layout, and `__main__.py`)
- Completion of Chapter 2 (values, types, `NoteDict`, `create_note`, `preview_note`, truthiness, and template strings)

Concept Overview

Programs are sequences of decisions. Control flow is the machinery behind them. Python provides conditionals, loops, and structural pattern matching to direct execution.

Conditionals rely on truthiness. Empty strings, zero, `None`, and empty collections evaluate to `False`; non-zero numbers and non-empty containers evaluate to `True`. For the CLI, this convention validates user input quickly. An empty title or body is falsy and can be rejected immediately.

Loops iterate over sequences or run while a condition holds. Python's `for` loop always walks an iterable. There is no C-style `for(i=0; i<n; i++)`. The `while` loop repeats as long as a condition stays true. Loop control statements (`break`, `continue`) and the loop `else` clause give precise control over iteration flow. The `else` block runs only when the loop terminates naturally, not via `break`.

Structural pattern matching provides `match` and `case` syntax for dispatching based on data shape. A wildcard `case _` catches unexpected values. For CLI routing, it replaces long `if/elif` chains with readable branches.

The standard library's `argparse` module turns command-line strings into structured data. Subparsers let a single entry point host multiple commands (`create`, `list`, `search`) without manual string splitting. Dashed option names such as `--source-url` become namespace attributes with underscores (`args.source_url`).

The Personal Knowledge Tracker CLI needs all of these. It must validate input, filter notes by tag, format output, and route parsed commands to the correct handler. Notes live only in memory for now. The process exits and the data disappears.

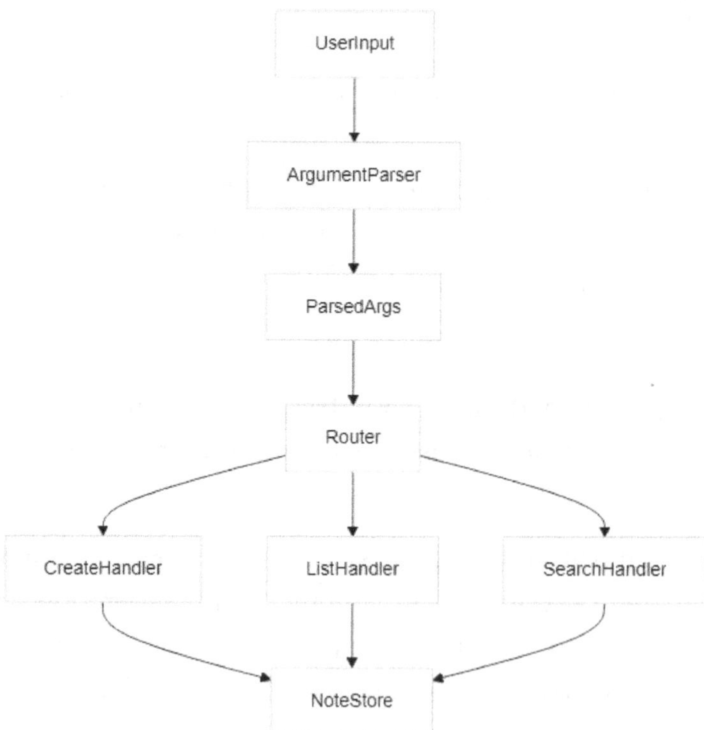

Step-by-Step Implementation

Step 1: Validate Notes and Check Tags with Truthiness

Before adding a note to the in-memory store, verify that it contains real data. The `is_valid_note` function checks that `title` and `body` are non-empty strings.

```
from knowledge_tracker.ch02_values import NoteDict

def is_valid_note(note: NoteDict) -> bool:
    title = note.get("title")
    body = note.get("body")
    return (
        isinstance(title, str)
        and isinstance(body, str)
        and title.strip() != ""
        and body.strip() != ""
    )
```

Bare truthiness accepts whitespace-only strings; always strip user input before validation. `isinstance` guards against non-string values, and `strip()` ensures the string contains more than spaces.

Next, implement tag membership. The `note_has_tag` function normalizes case and guards against malformed tag lists or individual non-string tags.

```
def note_has_tag(note: NoteDict, tag: str) -> bool:
    tags = note.get("tags")
    if not isinstance(tags, list):
        return False
    target = tag.lower()
    for t in tags:
        if isinstance(t, str) and t.lower() == target:
            return True
    return False
```

The `for` loop iterates over the tag list. Each tag is checked with `isinstance(t, str)` before comparing, so a `None` or numeric entry does not crash the function.

Step 2: Filter, Search, and Summarize with Loops

Filtering produces a new list of notes that match a criterion. The `filter_by_tag` function iterates over the store and collects matches.

```
def filter_by_tag(notes: list[NoteDict], tag: str) -> list[NoteDict]:
    results: list[NoteDict] = []
    for note in notes:
        if note_has_tag(note, tag):
            results.append(note)
    return results
```

Searching for a single note by title demonstrates `break` and loop `else`. The `else` clause runs only if the loop completed without hitting `break`.

```
from knowledge_tracker.ch02_values import preview_note

def find_note_by_title(notes: list[NoteDict], title: str) -> str:
    for note in notes:
        if not is_valid_note(note):
            continue
        if note.get("title") == title:
            result = preview_note(note)
            break
    else:
        return f"No note titled '{title}' found."
    return f"Found: {result}"
```

If the loop finds a match, `break` exits immediately and the `else` is skipped. If the iterable is exhausted naturally, `else` executes.

Summarization turns note dictionaries into readable lines. The `summarize_notes` function uses a `for` loop with `continue` to skip invalid notes. An optional `limit` parameter lets the caller stop early using `break`.

```
def summarize_notes(notes: list[NoteDict], limit: int | None = None)
-> str:
    lines: list[str] = []
    for note in notes:
        if not is_valid_note(note):
            continue
        lines.append(preview_note(note))
        if limit is not None and len(lines) >= limit:
            break
    if not lines:
        return "No notes found."
    return "\n".join(lines)
```

When `limit` is reached, `break` stops the loop. The final `if` after the loop handles the empty-results case.

A `while` loop is useful when you need index-based control. The `list_notes_with_limit` function demonstrates manual iteration with a counter.

```
def list_notes_with_limit(notes: list[NoteDict], limit: int) ->
list[str]:
    results: list[str] = []
    index = 0
    while index < len(notes):
        note = notes[index]
        if is_valid_note(note):
            results.append(preview_note(note))
            if len(results) >= limit:
                break
        index += 1
    return results
```

The `while` loop checks the index against the list length. It exits early via `break` once the limit is satisfied.

Step 3: Build the CLI Parser with argparse

A real CLI needs real parsing. The `argparse` module creates help text, validates required flags, and generates a namespace object. Subparsers give each command its own arguments.

```
import argparse

def build_parser() -> argparse.ArgumentParser:
    parser = argparse.ArgumentParser(
        prog="knowledge-tracker",
        description="Personal Knowledge Tracker CLI",
    )
    subparsers = parser.add_subparsers(dest="command", required=True)

    create_parser = subparsers.add_parser("create", help="Add a new
note")
    create_parser.add_argument("--title", required=True)
    create_parser.add_argument("--body", required=True)
    create_parser.add_argument("--tag", action="append", default=[])
    create_parser.add_argument("--source-url", default=None)

    list_parser = subparsers.add_parser("list", help="Show all
notes")
    list_parser.add_argument("--limit", type=int, default=None)

    search_parser = subparsers.add_parser("search", help="Find
notes")
```

```
    search_parser.add_argument("--tag", default=None)
    search_parser.add_argument("--query", default=None)

    return parser
```

Subparsers should always be required. Setting `required=True` on the subparser group forces the user to choose a command; without it, `args.command` would be `None`. I once traced a `NoneType` error for ten minutes before noticing the subparser group lacked `required=True`. The `action="append"` on `--tag` collects repeated flags into a list. `type=int` converts the `--limit` string to an integer. `default=None` leaves optional flags as `None` when omitted. Dashed option names such as `--source-url` become namespace attributes with underscores (`args.source_url`).

You can inspect the parsed namespace programmatically:

```
parser = build_parser()
args = parser.parse_args(["create", "--title", "Python 3.14", "--
body", "New features", "--tag", "cli"])
print(args.command)    # "create"
print(args.title)      # "Python 3.14"
print(args.tag)        # ["cli"]
print(args.source_url) # None
```

Step 4: Implement Command Handlers

Each subcommand maps to a handler function that receives the in-memory store and the parsed arguments. Handlers return strings; the caller prints them.

```
from knowledge_tracker.ch02_values import create_note, preview_note

def run_create(notes: list[NoteDict], args: argparse.Namespace) ->
str:
    if not args.title.strip() or not args.body.strip():
        return "Error: title and body cannot be empty."
    note = create_note(
        title=args.title,
        body=args.body,
        tags=args.tag,
        source_url=args.source_url,
    )
    if not is_valid_note(note):
        return "Error: note validation failed."
    notes.append(note)
```

```
    return f"Created note: {preview_note(note)}"

def run_list(notes: list[NoteDict], args: argparse.Namespace) -> str:
    if args.limit is not None:
        if args.limit <= 0:
            return "Error: limit must be a positive integer."
        return summarize_notes(notes, limit=args.limit)
    return summarize_notes(notes)

def run_search(notes: list[NoteDict], args: argparse.Namespace) ->
str:
    results = list(notes)
    if args.tag:
        results = filter_by_tag(results, args.tag)
    if args.query:
        query = args.query.lower()
        matched: list[NoteDict] = []
        for n in results:
            title = str(n.get("title", "")).lower()
            body = str(n.get("body", "")).lower()
            source = str(n.get("source_url") or "").lower()
            if query in title or query in body or query in source:
                matched.append(n)
        results = matched
    return summarize_notes(results)
```

`run_create` strips whitespace before checking truthiness. `run_list` rejects non-positive limits. `run_search` defensively copies `notes` with `list(notes)` so filtering does not mutate the original store. The explicit `for` loop checks title, body, and source URL for the query substring.

Step 5: Route Commands with match and case

The `route` function dispatches to the correct handler using structural pattern matching. This is cleaner than a chain of `if args.command == "create"` statements.

```
def route(notes: list[NoteDict], args: argparse.Namespace) -> str:
    match args.command:
        case "create":
            return run_create(notes, args)
        case "list":
            return run_list(notes, args)
        case "search":
            return run_search(notes, args)
        case _:
            return f"Unknown command: {args.command}"
```

The wildcard `case _` catches unexpected values. Because `argparse` enforces valid subcommands, this branch is defensive.

Step 6: Wire Everything in the CLI Entry Point

The `run_cli` function serves as the entry point for the tracker CLI. It instantiates the parser, allocates an in-memory store seeded with sample notes, and prints the routed result.

```
def run_cli() -> None:
    parser = build_parser()
    args = parser.parse_args()

    # Ephemeral store: data exists only for the lifetime of this
process.
    notes: list[NoteDict] = [
        create_note("Python 3.14 Features", "Template strings and
more", ["python", "news"]),
        create_note("uv Workflow", "Fast dependency resolution with
uv", ["tooling", "uv"]),
    ]

    output = route(notes, args)
    print(output)
```

Process-local state is acceptable for a tutorial; it is unacceptable for a real tool. Seed data lets you test `list` and `search` right away. Once the process exits, the local list vanishes. Chapter 6 will replace this with file persistence.

Run the module from the project root using the package path:

```
uv run python -m knowledge_tracker.ch03_control_flow create --title
"Python 3.14" --body "New features" --tag cli
uv run python -m knowledge_tracker.ch03_control_flow list
uv run python -m knowledge_tracker.ch03_control_flow search --query
"uv"
```

Full Example

Below is the complete `ch03_control_flow.py` module. It repeats the `NoteDict` alias and Chapter 2 helpers so that the file is runnable in isolation without cross-module imports.

```
# ch03_control_flow.py
"""Control flow and CLI routing for the Personal Knowledge
Tracker."""

import argparse
from datetime import datetime, timezone

# -------------------------------------------------------------------
----------
# Carried forward from Chapter 2
# -------------------------------------------------------------------
----------
type NoteDict = dict[str, str | list[str] | None]

def create_note(
    title: str,
    body: str,
    tags: list[str],
    source_url: str | None = None,
) -> NoteDict:
    return {
        "title": title,
        "body": body,
        "tags": tags,
        "created": datetime.now(timezone.utc).isoformat(),
        "source_url": source_url,
    }

def preview_note(note: NoteDict) -> str:
    title = note.get("title") or ""
    tags = note.get("tags")
    if not isinstance(tags, list):
        tags = []
    tag_str = ", ".join(f"#{t}" for t in tags)
    return f"{title} [{tag_str}]"

# -------------------------------------------------------------------
----------
# Chapter 3: validation, filtering, and search
# -------------------------------------------------------------------
----------
def is_valid_note(note: NoteDict) -> bool:
    title = note.get("title")
    body = note.get("body")
    return (
        isinstance(title, str)
        and isinstance(body, str)
        and title.strip() != ""
        and body.strip() != ""
    )

def note_has_tag(note: NoteDict, tag: str) -> bool:
    tags = note.get("tags")
    if not isinstance(tags, list):
```

```
        return False
    target = tag.lower()
    for t in tags:
        if isinstance(t, str) and t.lower() == target:
            return True
    return False

def filter_by_tag(notes: list[NoteDict], tag: str) -> list[NoteDict]:
    results: list[NoteDict] = []
    for note in notes:
        if note_has_tag(note, tag):
            results.append(note)
    return results

def find_note_by_title(notes: list[NoteDict], title: str) -> str:
    for note in notes:
        if not is_valid_note(note):
            continue
        if note.get("title") == title:
            result = preview_note(note)
            break
    else:
        return f"No note titled '{title}' found."
    return f"Found: {result}"

def summarize_notes(notes: list[NoteDict], limit: int | None = None)
-> str:
    lines: list[str] = []
    for note in notes:
        if not is_valid_note(note):
            continue
        lines.append(preview_note(note))
        if limit is not None and len(lines) >= limit:
            break
    if not lines:
        return "No notes found."
    return "\n".join(lines)

def list_notes_with_limit(notes: list[NoteDict], limit: int) ->
list[str]:
    results: list[str] = []
    index = 0
    while index < len(notes):
        note = notes[index]
        if is_valid_note(note):
            results.append(preview_note(note))
            if len(results) >= limit:
                break
        index += 1
    return results

# ----------------------------------------------------------------------
----------
# Chapter 3: CLI parsing and routing
```

```
# ------------------------------------------------------------
----------
def build_parser() -> argparse.ArgumentParser:
    parser = argparse.ArgumentParser(
        prog="knowledge-tracker",
        description="Personal Knowledge Tracker CLI",
    )
    subparsers = parser.add_subparsers(dest="command", required=True)

    create_parser = subparsers.add_parser("create", help="Add a new
note")
    create_parser.add_argument("--title", required=True)
    create_parser.add_argument("--body", required=True)
    create_parser.add_argument("--tag", action="append", default=[])
    create_parser.add_argument("--source-url", default=None)

    list_parser = subparsers.add_parser("list", help="Show all
notes")
    list_parser.add_argument("--limit", type=int, default=None)

    search_parser = subparsers.add_parser("search", help="Find
notes")
    search_parser.add_argument("--tag", default=None)
    search_parser.add_argument("--query", default=None)

    return parser

def run_create(notes: list[NoteDict], args: argparse.Namespace) ->
str:
    if not args.title.strip() or not args.body.strip():
        return "Error: title and body cannot be empty."
    note = create_note(
        title=args.title,
        body=args.body,
        tags=args.tag,
        source_url=args.source_url,
    )
    if not is_valid_note(note):
        return "Error: note validation failed."
    notes.append(note)
    return f"Created note: {preview_note(note)}"

def run_list(notes: list[NoteDict], args: argparse.Namespace) -> str:
    if args.limit is not None:
        if args.limit <= 0:
            return "Error: limit must be a positive integer."
        return summarize_notes(notes, limit=args.limit)
    return summarize_notes(notes)

def run_search(notes: list[NoteDict], args: argparse.Namespace) ->
str:
    results = list(notes)
    if args.tag:
        results = filter_by_tag(results, args.tag)
```

```
    if args.query:
        query = args.query.lower()
        matched: list[NoteDict] = []
        for n in results:
            title = str(n.get("title", "")).lower()
            body = str(n.get("body", "")).lower()
            source = str(n.get("source_url") or "").lower()
            if query in title or query in body or query in source:
                matched.append(n)
        results = matched
    return summarize_notes(results)

def route(notes: list[NoteDict], args: argparse.Namespace) -> str:
    match args.command:
        case "create":
            return run_create(notes, args)
        case "list":
            return run_list(notes, args)
        case "search":
            return run_search(notes, args)
        case _:
            return f"Unknown command: {args.command}"

def run_cli() -> None:
    parser = build_parser()
    args = parser.parse_args()

    notes: list[NoteDict] = [
        create_note("Python 3.14 Features", "Template strings and
more", ["python", "news"]),
        create_note("uv Workflow", "Fast dependency resolution with
uv", ["tooling", "uv"]),
    ]

    output = route(notes, args)
    print(output)

if __name__ == "__main__":
    run_cli()
```

The module is self-contained. It defines the data shape, validation logic, filtering, search, summarization, argument parsing, command handlers, and routing in one file. This layout is suitable for learning; Chapter 7 will split it into a package.

Common Mistakes

- **Using `is` for value equality.** `is` checks identity, not equality. Use `==` to compare strings and numbers. Use `is` only for singletons such as `None`, `True`, and `False`.
- **Writing `if x == True:` instead of `if x:`.** Explicit comparison to `True` is redundant and fails when `x` is a non-boolean truthy value such as a non-empty string.
- **Expecting loop `else` to run on `break`.** The `else` clause on a `for` or `while` loop executes only when the loop terminates naturally, not when it exits through `break`. If you need logic after a break, place it after the loop body.
- **Forgetting that empty collections are falsy.** A check like `if tags:` is sufficient to reject `None`, empty lists, and missing keys. Do not write `if tags is not None and len(tags) > 0:` unless you truly need to distinguish `None` from `[]`.
- **Calling `parser.parse_args()` without capturing the result.** The function returns a namespace; assign it to a variable before inspecting arguments.
- **Shadowing built-in names.** Naming a variable `list` or `dict` overrides the built-in type and causes subtle failures later in the same scope. Use `results` or `notes_list` instead.
- **Omitting `required=True` on subparsers.** Without this flag, `argparse` allows invocation with no subcommand, leaving `args.command` as `None` and forcing manual validation.
- **Trusting truthiness alone for user input.** An all-whitespace string is truthy. Always `strip()` strings that come from CLI arguments before validating them.
- **Allowing non-positive numeric limits.** A `--limit` of `0` or `-1` produces confusing output. Reject values that are not strictly positive.

Performance and Production Considerations

The in-memory `list[NoteDict]` store is acceptable for learning and small datasets. Data disappears when the process exits; Chapter 6 will introduce file persistence with `pathlib` and JSON.

Linear search through notes is O(n) for both listing and tag filtering. A personal tracker with hundreds of notes will not feel this cost. Do not optimize with indexing until profiling proves it necessary.

`argparse` is the right choice for this scale. Third-party libraries such as `click` or `typer` add dependencies and indirection that are not justified for three subcommands. Stick with the standard library until the CLI grows significantly.

`match/case` dispatch compiles to efficient bytecode and is preferable to long `if/elif` chains for command routing. The visual structure makes it easier for humans to spot missing branches, though Python static analyzers do not enforce exhaustiveness for string patterns.

The `summarize_notes` function materializes all lines in memory before joining them. For very large note stores, yield lines from a generator and stream them to stdout. The current implementation prioritizes clarity over streaming.

Summary

Control flow directs every program decision. Python's truthiness rules eliminate boilerplate comparisons, but user input still requires explicit type and whitespace checks. `if`, `elif`, and `else` handle branching. `for` and `while` loops process collections, with `break`, `continue`, and loop `else` providing fine-grained control. Structural pattern matching with `match` and `case` offers readable dispatch for CLI commands.

The Personal Knowledge Tracker CLI now parses real arguments through `argparse`, routes subcommands via `match/case`, and manipulates an in-memory note store with validated, filtered, and summarized output. The store is seeded for immediate testing and is intentionally ephemeral; Chapter 6 will replace it with disk persistence, and Chapter 7 will refactor these functions into a package structure.

Key Terms

- **Truthiness**: The boolean evaluation of objects in Python, where empty collections, zero numeric values, and `None` resolve to `False`, while non-empty collections and non-zero values resolve to `True`.
- **Membership test**: An expression using the `in` operator to check whether a value exists within a collection or iterable.
- **Loop `else`**: A clause on `for` and `while` loops that executes only when the loop terminates naturally, not via `break`.
- **Structural pattern matching**: The `match` and `case` syntax for dispatching execution based on data shape and value.
- **`argparse`**: The standard library module for parsing command-line arguments and generating help text.
- **Subparsers**: Components of an `ArgumentParser` that allow a single CLI entry point to host multiple distinct commands with their own flags.
- **Command handler**: A function that receives parsed arguments and application state, then executes the logic for a specific CLI subcommand.
- **Wildcard pattern**: The `case _` pattern in a `match` statement that matches any value not caught by preceding cases.

Mini Quiz

1. **You add a new `delete` handler inside `route` but forget to register a `delete` subparser in `build_parser`. What happens when a user runs `knowledge-tracker delete`?**

   A. `argparse` rejects the command because `delete` is not a recognized subcommand

   B. The `case _` pattern catches it and prints "Unknown command"

   C. Python raises a `KeyError` when accessing `args.command`

   D. The program executes the `delete` handler anyway

2. **Look at the `summarize_notes` function. If `notes` contains two items, one valid and one invalid, what does the function return?**

   A. "No notes found."

   B. An empty string

   C. A string containing both notes

   D. Only the preview string for the valid note

3. **Which expression is the idiomatic way to check whether a note has tags using Python truthiness?**

   A. `if note.get("tags") is not None:`

   B. `if note.get("tags") == True:`

   C. `if note.get("tags"):`

   D. `if bool(note.get("tags")) is True:`

4. **In `note_has_tag`, what happens when a note's `tags` field is `None`?**

   A. The function returns `False` because `None` is not a list

   B. The function raises a `TypeError`

   C. The `in` operator converts `None` to an empty list

   D. The generator expression produces an infinite loop

5. **What is the main benefit of using `match` and `case` instead of a long `if`/`elif` chain for CLI routing?**

   A. It avoids importing the `argparse` module

   B. It automatically validates that all subcommands have handlers

C. It makes value-based dispatch explicit and keeps command routing readable as the CLI grows

D. It executes significantly faster than `if/elif`

6. **Which configuration ensures that `argparse` rejects invocation when no subcommand is provided?**

   A. `parser.add_subparsers(dest="command")`

   B. `subparsers.add_parser("create", required=True)`

   C. `parser.add_argument("command", required=True)`

   D. `parser.add_subparsers(dest="command", required=True)`

Answers are provided in the Answer Key at the end of the book.

Activity

Extend the Personal Knowledge Tracker CLI with a `stats` subcommand that reports the total number of notes and the frequency of each tag.

- Open `src/knowledge_tracker/ch03_control_flow.py` and locate `build_parser`.
- Add a new subparser named `stats` with `help="Show tag statistics"`.
- Implement `run_stats(notes: list[NoteDict], args: argparse.Namespace) -> str` above the `route` function.
- Count the total notes using `len(notes)`.
- Use a dictionary to accumulate tag frequencies by iterating over all notes and their tags.
- Skip notes where `tags` is not a list.
- Return a formatted string with the total count and each tag with its frequency, sorted alphabetically by tag name.
- Add `case "stats":` to the `match` block inside `route` and return `run_stats(notes, args)`.
- Temporarily seed the `notes` list at module level with two or three sample notes so you can test without persistent storage.
- Run `uv run python -m knowledge_tracker.ch03_control_flow stats` and confirm the output shows correct totals and tag counts.

Use this skeleton for `run_stats`:

```
def run_stats(notes: list[NoteDict], args: argparse.Namespace) ->
str:
    if not notes:
        return "No notes found."

    tag_counts: dict[str, int] = {}
    for note in notes:
        tags = note.get("tags")
        if not isinstance(tags, list):
            continue
        for tag in tags:
            if isinstance(tag, str):
                tag_counts[tag] = tag_counts.get(tag, 0) + 1

    lines: list[str] = [f"Total notes: {len(notes)}"]
    for tag in sorted(tag_counts):
        lines.append(f"  #{tag}: {tag_counts[tag]}")
```

```
    return "\n".join(lines)
```

Part II: Core Language

Chapter 4: Functions, Scope, and Deferred Annotations

What You Will Learn

- Write functions with explicit type hints, return annotations, and keyword-only parameters
- Avoid the mutable default argument pitfall by using `None` and conditional initialization
- Predict name resolution behavior across local and module scopes
- Retrieve and evaluate deferred annotations using `annotationlib.get_annotations` and the `Format` enum in Python 3.14
- Apply template strings to build context-aware, safely escaped renderings of note data
- Decompose CLI workflows into small, testable functions with clear contracts

Prerequisites

- Completion of Chapter 1 (project setup with `uv`, source layout, and running scripts)
- Understanding of values, types, strings, `NoteDict`, and template string basics from Chapter 2
- Understanding of control flow, truthiness, `argparse` routing, and in-memory note filtering from Chapter 3

Concept Overview

Functions are Python's primary unit of reuse. A function definition creates a callable object, binds default expressions at definition time, and introduces a local namespace every time it is invoked. Type hints describe the contract, but the runtime remains dynamically typed; annotations are stored and optionally inspected by tools.

Python 3.14 changes how annotations are evaluated. PEP 649 introduces deferred annotation evaluation by default. Annotations are no longer eagerly executed at class or function definition time. Instead, the runtime stores them lazily and resolves each value on first access, which eliminates the need for forward-reference quotes in many cases. Annotations are not evaluated until they are accessed. In the majority of cases code continues to work as-is; `__annotations__` still returns a normal dict. When you need to control how unresolved names are handled, use the new `annotationlib` module with `get_annotations(obj, format=Format.VALUE)`.

The Personal Knowledge Tracker CLI benefits directly from these mechanics. Note creation, HTML preview generation, and advanced search are each natural candidates for small, single-purpose functions. Keyword-only arguments make the public API harder to misuse. Safe defaults prevent shared state bugs. Template strings keep rendering pipelines explicit. Deferred annotations keep the codebase clean as the data model grows.

Step-by-Step Implementation

Step 1: Module Constants, Defaults, and Safe Truncation

Default argument expressions are evaluated once, when the `def` statement executes. They live in the module scope. The following constant and two functions demonstrate safe truncation and tag formatting for note previews.

```
DEFAULT_PREVIEW_WIDTH: int = 40

def truncate_title_advanced(title: str, width: int =
DEFAULT_PREVIEW_WIDTH) -> str:
    if width < 3:
        return title[:width]
    if len(title) <= width:
        return title
    return title[: width - 3] + "..."

def format_tag_line(tags: list[str]) -> str:
    if not tags:
        return "No tags"
    formatted: list[str] = []
    for t in tags:
        formatted.append(f"#{t.lower()}")
    return " ".join(formatted)
```

`truncate_title_advanced` uses the module constant as its default. Callers may override `width` positionally or by name, which keeps the calling convention explicit. `format_tag_line` produces a space-separated tag string suitable for HTML footers. Both functions are pure. The loop in `format_tag_line` avoids list-comprehension syntax, which Chapter 5 covers in depth.

Step 2: Keyword-Only Arguments and the Mutable Default Bug

Python allows you to force arguments to be passed by name. Place a bare `*` in the parameter list; everything after it becomes keyword-only. This is ideal for options that affect behavior but should never be confused with positional data.

The following `build_note_id` function generates a stable identifier from a note title. The `prefix` parameter is keyword-only. The timestamp includes microseconds to reduce the chance of collision during rapid successive calls.

```
from datetime import datetime, timezone
from knowledge_tracker.ch02_values import NoteDict, create_note

def build_note_id(title: str, *, prefix: str = "note") -> str:
    safe = "".join(c if c.isalnum() else "_" for c in title.lower())
    timestamp = datetime.now(timezone.utc).strftime("%Y%m%d%H%M%S%f")
    return f"{prefix}-{safe}-{timestamp}"
```

Because `prefix` follows `*`, a call like `build_note_id("Hello", "hw")` raises `TypeError`. Callers must write `build_note_id("Hello", prefix="hw")`. This prevents accidental positional passes during refactoring.

Now consider defaults. The classic mutable default bug strikes when a list or dictionary is used as a default value. The object is created once at definition time and shared across every call that omits the argument.

```
def collect_tags_wrong(tags: list[str] = []) -> list[str]:
    return tags
```

Mutable default arguments are the most common source of subtle bugs in Python functions.

The bug manifests immediately. The following demonstration shows how a mutation in one call survives into the next.

```
def demo_mutable_default_bug() -> None:
```

```
    first = collect_tags_wrong()
    first.append("python")
    second = collect_tags_wrong()
    print(f"Mutable default bug: second call sees {second}")
```

The corrected pattern uses `None` as the default, initializes a fresh list inside the function, and returns a copy so callers cannot mutate internal state.

```
def collect_tags_safe(tags: list[str] | None = None) -> list[str]:
    return list(tags) if tags is not None else []
```

`safe_create_note` wraps the original `create_note` from Chapter 2. It avoids the shared list bug by copying the caller's tags, validates nothing implicitly, and attaches a generated `id` field to the resulting dictionary. This is a transitional step; Chapter 8 replaces dictionary-based notes with dataclasses.

```
def safe_create_note(
    title: str,
    body: str,
    tags: list[str] | None = None,
    source_url: str | None = None,
) -> NoteDict:
    resolved_tags = list(tags) if tags is not None else []
    note = create_note(title=title, body=body, tags=resolved_tags,
source_url=source_url)
    note["id"] = build_note_id(title, prefix="note")
    return note
```

Step 3: Template Strings for Safe HTML Rendering

Chapter 2 introduced template strings with `t"..."`. Unlike f-strings, t-strings produce a `string.templatelib.Template` object whose interpolations can be escaped before rendering. The following function renders a note as HTML by constructing a template and passing it through the safe renderer. It also validates that any `source_url` uses an expected scheme before emitting an anchor tag.

```
from knowledge_tracker.ch02_values import render_safe_html

def render_note_html(note: NoteDict) -> str:
    title = note.get("title", "")
    body = note.get("body", "")
    tags = note.get("tags", [])
```

```
    source = note.get("source_url")
    if not isinstance(tags, list):
        tags = []
    tag_str = format_tag_line(tags)
    safe_source = ""
    if isinstance(source, str) and source.startswith(("http://",
"https://")):
        safe_source = source
    if safe_source:
        template = t'<article><h2>{title}</h2><p>{body}</p><a
href="{safe_source}">Source</a><footer>{tag_str}</footer></article>'
    else:
        template =
t'<article><h2>{title}</h2><p>{body}</p><footer>{tag_str}</footer></a
rticle>'
    return render_safe_html(template)
```

The static HTML structure lives in the template literal. The dynamic parts are captured as `Interpolation` instances. `render_safe_html` escapes each interpolation value, so a title containing `<script>` cannot inject markup. This is structural safety, not automatic safety; the escape policy lives in the renderer, not the literal. I once found XSS in a service that rendered user titles with f-strings. Links are rendered only for recognized HTTP schemes to avoid unsafe `javascript:` or `data:` URLs in the output.

Step 4: Deferred Annotation Evaluation and Advanced Search

Python 3.14 evaluates annotations lazily. When you define a function with type hints, the runtime stores them in a deferred form and resolves each value the first time it is read. Accessing `__annotations__` directly still returns a normal working dict; you get real annotation objects, not unresolved proxies. The modern, format-aware way to read annotations is the new `annotationlib` module, which lets you choose how undefined names are handled.

```
from annotationlib import get_annotations, Format
```

`get_annotations` accepts a `format=` keyword whose value is a `Format` enum member:

- `Format.VALUE` returns the real runtime values, the same objects you would get by evaluating each annotation.

- `Format.FORWARDREF` returns values where any undefined name becomes a `ForwardRef` marker instead of raising `NameError`.
- `Format.STRING` returns each annotation as its source string.

`inspect.get_annotations()` and `typing.get_type_hints()` still work for resolving annotations, but `annotationlib` is the modern format-aware path in 3.14.

The following search function carries rich hints. Its annotations include forward-friendly constructs such as `list[NoteDict]` and `| None` unions. An early guard rejects non-positive `limit` values to avoid unnecessary work.

```
from annotationlib import get_annotations, Format
from knowledge_tracker.ch03_control_flow import note_has_tag

def search_notes_advanced(
    notes: list[NoteDict],
    query: str,
    *,
    require_all_tags: list[str] | None = None,
    limit: int | None = None,
) -> list[NoteDict]:
    if limit is not None and limit <= 0:
        return []
    results: list[NoteDict] = []
    q = query.lower()
    for note in notes:
        if not isinstance(note, dict):
            continue
        title = note.get("title", "")
        body = note.get("body", "")
        src = note.get("source_url", "")
        text = f"{title} {body} {src}".lower()
        if q not in text:
            continue
        if require_all_tags:
            tags = note.get("tags", [])
            if not isinstance(tags, list):
                continue
            missing = False
            for t in require_all_tags:
                if not note_has_tag(note, t):
                    missing = True
                    break
            if missing:
                continue
        results.append(note)
        if limit is not None and len(results) >= limit:
            break
    return results
```

To read these annotations in 3.14, wrap `annotationlib.get_annotations` and request resolved values.

```
def inspect_annotations(func: object) -> dict[str, object]:
    return get_annotations(func, format=Format.VALUE)
```

Evaluating `inspect_annotations(search_notes_advanced)` returns a dictionary mapping parameter names to resolved types such as `list[NoteDict]` and `str`. `Format.VALUE` gives you the real objects; switch to `Format.FORWARDREF` when an annotation may reference a name that is not yet defined, or `Format.STRING` when you only need the source text.

Step 5: Local Scope and Name Shadowing

When a name is assigned inside a function, Python treats it as local. That local binding shadows any module-level name of the same identifier. Defaults are unaffected. They bind at definition time in the module scope.

```
def demo_scope(title: str = "Shadow Demo") -> str:
    DEFAULT_PREVIEW_WIDTH = 10
    return truncate_title_advanced(title, DEFAULT_PREVIEW_WIDTH)
```

Inside `demo_scope`, `DEFAULT_PREVIEW_WIDTH` is a new local variable. The call to `truncate_title_advanced` passes it explicitly as the `width` argument. If we called `truncate_title_advanced(title)` without the second argument, the default expression would still resolve to the module constant `40`, not the local `10`. Defaults are frozen at definition time; they do not dynamically lookup names in the caller's scope.

Step 6: Composing the Tracker Workflow

The following command handler composes `search_notes_advanced` with `preview_note` to produce a reusable, CLI-friendly entry point. It accepts discrete parameters that mirror parsed command line flags.

```
from knowledge_tracker.ch02_values import preview_note

def run_advanced_search(
    notes: list[NoteDict],
    query: str,
    *,
```

```
    tags: list[str] | None = None,
    limit: int | None = None,
) -> str:
    results = search_notes_advanced(notes, query,
require_all_tags=tags, limit=limit)
    if not results:
        return "No notes found"
    lines: list[str] = []
    for note in results:
        lines.append(preview_note(note))
    return "\n".join(lines)
```

The integration function below exercises every new abstraction in sequence. It demonstrates scope behavior, the mutable default bug, safe note creation, HTML rendering, deferred annotation inspection, keyword-only calling conventions, and the advanced search handler.

```
def run_functions_demo() -> None:
    print("=== Functions, Scope, and Deferred Annotations Demo ===")

    print("Scope demo:", demo_scope())

    demo_mutable_default_bug()

    note = safe_create_note(
        title="Deferred Annotations in 3.14",
        body="PEP 649 changes when annotations are resolved.",
        tags=["python", "pep"],
    )
    print(f"Note ID: {note.get('id')}")
    print("HTML:", render_note_html(note))

    print("Annotations:", inspect_annotations(search_notes_advanced))
    print("Keyword-only ID:", build_note_id("Hello World",
prefix="hw"))

    sample_notes: list[NoteDict] = [
        note,
        safe_create_note("Second Note", "Body two", ["pep"]),
    ]
    print("Advanced search:", run_advanced_search(sample_notes,
"pep", tags=["pep"]))
```

Run the module with uv `run python -m knowledge_tracker.ch04_functions`. Typical output looks like this:

```
=== Functions, Scope, and Deferred Annotations Demo ===
Scope demo: Shadow ...
```

```
Mutable default bug: second call sees ['python']
Note ID: note-deferred_annotations_in_314-20251007120000000000
HTML: <article><h2>Deferred Annotations in 3.14</h2><p>PEP 649
changes when annotations are resolved.</p><footer>#python
#pep</footer></article>
Annotations: {'notes': list[NoteDict], 'query': <class 'str'>, ...}
Keyword-only ID: hw-hello_world-20251007120000000000
Advanced search: Deferred Annotations in 3.14 [#python, #pep]
```

Full Example

The complete `ch04_functions.py` module combines all steps into one runnable file. It imports helpers from Chapters 2 and 3 and defines new functions for truncation, identification, safe creation, HTML rendering, advanced search, annotation inspection, scope demonstration, and a composed search handler.

```
from annotationlib import get_annotations, Format
from datetime import datetime, timezone

from knowledge_tracker.ch02_values import NoteDict, create_note,
preview_note, render_safe_html
from knowledge_tracker.ch03_control_flow import note_has_tag

DEFAULT_PREVIEW_WIDTH: int = 40

def truncate_title_advanced(title: str, width: int =
DEFAULT_PREVIEW_WIDTH) -> str:
    if width < 3:
        return title[:width]
    if len(title) <= width:
        return title
    return title[: width - 3] + "..."

def format_tag_line(tags: list[str]) -> str:
    if not tags:
        return "No tags"
    formatted: list[str] = []
    for t in tags:
        formatted.append(f"#{t.lower()}")
    return " ".join(formatted)

def build_note_id(title: str, *, prefix: str = "note") -> str:
    safe = "".join(c if c.isalnum() else "_" for c in title.lower())
    timestamp = datetime.now(timezone.utc).strftime("%Y%m%d%H%M%S%f")
    return f"{prefix}-{safe}-{timestamp}"

def collect_tags_wrong(tags: list[str] = []) -> list[str]:  # noqa:
B006
    """Intentionally wrong: demonstrates the mutable default bug."""
```

```
    return tags

def demo_mutable_default_bug() -> None:
    first = collect_tags_wrong()
    first.append("python")
    second = collect_tags_wrong()
    print(f"Mutable default bug: second call sees {second}")

def collect_tags_safe(tags: list[str] | None = None) -> list[str]:
    return list(tags) if tags is not None else []

def safe_create_note(
    title: str,
    body: str,
    tags: list[str] | None = None,
    source_url: str | None = None,
) -> NoteDict:
    resolved_tags = list(tags) if tags is not None else []
    note = create_note(title=title, body=body, tags=resolved_tags,
source_url=source_url)
    note["id"] = build_note_id(title, prefix="note")
    return note

def render_note_html(note: NoteDict) -> str:
    title = note.get("title", "")
    body = note.get("body", "")
    tags = note.get("tags", [])
    source = note.get("source_url")
    if not isinstance(tags, list):
        tags = []
    tag_str = format_tag_line(tags)
    safe_source = ""
    if isinstance(source, str) and source.startswith(("http://",
"https://")):
        safe_source = source
    if safe_source:
        template = t'<article><h2>{title}</h2><p>{body}</p><a
href="{safe_source}">Source</a><footer>{tag_str}</footer></article>'
    else:
        template =
t'<article><h2>{title}</h2><p>{body}</p><footer>{tag_str}</footer></a
rticle>'
    return render_safe_html(template)

def search_notes_advanced(
    notes: list[NoteDict],
    query: str,
    *,
    require_all_tags: list[str] | None = None,
    limit: int | None = None,
) -> list[NoteDict]:
    if limit is not None and limit <= 0:
        return []
    results: list[NoteDict] = []
```

```
    q = query.lower()
    for note in notes:
        if not isinstance(note, dict):
            continue
        title = note.get("title", "")
        body = note.get("body", "")
        src = note.get("source_url", "")
        text = f"{title} {body} {src}".lower()
        if q not in text:
            continue
        if require_all_tags:
            tags = note.get("tags", [])
            if not isinstance(tags, list):
                continue
            missing = False
            for t in require_all_tags:
                if not note_has_tag(note, t):
                    missing = True
                    break
            if missing:
                continue
        results.append(note)
        if limit is not None and len(results) >= limit:
            break
    return results

def inspect_annotations(func: object) -> dict[str, object]:
    return get_annotations(func, format=Format.VALUE)

def demo_scope(title: str = "Shadow Demo") -> str:
    DEFAULT_PREVIEW_WIDTH = 10
    return truncate_title_advanced(title, DEFAULT_PREVIEW_WIDTH)

def run_advanced_search(
    notes: list[NoteDict],
    query: str,
    *,
    tags: list[str] | None = None,
    limit: int | None = None,
) -> str:
    results = search_notes_advanced(notes, query,
require_all_tags=tags, limit=limit)
    if not results:
        return "No notes found"
    lines: list[str] = []
    for note in results:
        lines.append(preview_note(note))
    return "\n".join(lines)

def run_functions_demo() -> None:
    print("=== Functions, Scope, and Deferred Annotations Demo ===")

    print("Scope demo:", demo_scope())
```

```
    demo_mutable_default_bug()

    note = safe_create_note(
        title="Deferred Annotations in 3.14",
        body="PEP 649 changes when annotations are resolved.",
        tags=["python", "pep"],
    )
    print(f"Note ID: {note.get('id')}")
    print("HTML:", render_note_html(note))

    print("Annotations:", inspect_annotations(search_notes_advanced))
    print("Keyword-only ID:", build_note_id("Hello World",
prefix="hw"))

    sample_notes: list[NoteDict] = [
        note,
        safe_create_note("Second Note", "Body two", ["pep"]),
    ]
    print("Advanced search:", run_advanced_search(sample_notes,
"pep", tags=["pep"]))

if __name__ == "__main__":
    run_functions_demo()
```

This module keeps the Personal Knowledge Tracker CLI evolving without overbuilding. `safe_create_note` layers an ID and a copied tag list on top of the existing `create_note`. `render_note_html` reuses the safe HTML pipeline from Chapter 2 and validates URL schemes. Keyword-only arguments in `search_notes_advanced` expose tag filtering and result limits. `run_advanced_search` wraps the new search logic into a handler that returns printable output. The entire file is runnable. It demonstrates Python 3.14 deferred annotations through `inspect_annotations`, which reads resolved values via `annotationlib.get_annotations(..., format=Format.VALUE)`.

Common Mistakes

- **Using mutable defaults such as `[]` or `{}` in parameter lists.** Default expressions execute once at definition time. A shared list accumulates mutations across calls. I once debugged a production cache corrupted by a default list that accumulated state across requests. Initialize mutable collections inside the function body using `None` as the default.
- **Shadowing module constants unintentionally.** Assigning to a name inside a function creates a local binding that hides the module-

level object. This is safe when intentional, yet confusing when accidental. Use distinct local names to avoid ambiguity.

- **Assuming `__annotations__` is broken in Python 3.14.** PEP 649 makes annotations lazy, but `__annotations__` still returns a normal working dict with real values resolved on access. In the majority of cases reading it directly is fine. When you need to control undefined-name handling or pick a specific output format, use `annotationlib.get_annotations(obj, format=Format.VALUE)` (or `Format.FORWARDREF` / `Format.STRING`).
- **Omitting ` before `keyword-only parameters.** Without the bare` *`, callers can still pass optional flags positionally. This reduces clarity and increases fragility during API changes. Force keyword-only calling for every optional behavioral flag.
- **Assuming default arguments re-evaluate on every call.** A default like `datetime.now()` captures the moment of function definition, not the moment of invocation. Move dynamic default logic into the function body.

Performance and Production Considerations

- `search_notes_advanced` scans the entire note list for every call. This is O(n) and unavoidable for a linear search, but the early `limit <= 0` guard and the `limit` break prevent wasted work. For large stores, avoid repeated full scans by building indexes (covered in Chapter 5).
- `render_note_html` allocates a `Template` object and escapes every interpolation. This is safer than f-strings for user-facing output, but it costs extra allocations. Use t-strings for rendered HTML; use f-strings for internal diagnostics where no escaping is required.
- `build_note_id` includes microsecond precision to reduce collisions in normal CLI usage. If you distribute the tracker across processes, replace the timestamp with `uuid.uuid4().hex` for stronger uniqueness guarantees.
- `safe_create_note` copies the caller's tag list with `list(tags)`. This prevents accidental mutation of the caller's data. The copy is O(k) for k tags; negligible for small lists, but part of the function's contract that callers should know about.

Summary

Functions in Python are flexible contracts. Type hints document intent without enforcing it at runtime. Default arguments bind at definition time, so mutable objects must be initialized inside the function body. Keyword-only parameters, enforced with `*`, make APIs self-documenting and resistant to breakage. Local assignments shadow module names, but default expressions remain anchored to the module scope where the function was defined.

Python 3.14 changes how annotations are stored. Deferred evaluation eliminates forward-reference quoting in most cases, since annotations are not evaluated until they are accessed. `__annotations__` still returns a working dict, so most code keeps running unchanged; when you need format control, retrieve annotations with `annotationlib.get_annotations(..., format=Format.VALUE)`. Template strings keep rendering pipelines explicit and safe by separating structure from escaping logic.

The Personal Knowledge Tracker CLI now generates stable note IDs, renders escaped HTML previews, and performs advanced filtered searches. Each operation lives in a small, testable function. In Chapter 5, these functions will operate on collections, streams, and iterators to handle larger note stores without loading more data than necessary.

Key Terms

This chapter introduced the following terms related to functions, scope, and Python 3.14 annotations.

- **Deferred annotation evaluation**: PEP 649 behavior in Python 3.14 that stores type hints lazily and resolves them on demand rather than at definition time.
- **Keyword-only argument**: A parameter placed after a bare `*` in a function signature, forcing callers to pass it by name.
- **Mutable default argument**: A list, dictionary, or other mutable object used as a parameter default, which creates shared state across function calls.
- **Name shadowing**: When a local variable binding hides a module-level or outer-scope name of the same identifier.

- **Pure function**: A function that depends only on its inputs and produces no side effects or mutations of external state.
- **`annotationlib.get_annotations`**: The modern Python 3.14 API for retrieving function, class, or module annotations, with a `format=` keyword (`Format.VALUE`, `Format.FORWARDREF`, `Format.STRING`) controlling how values are returned.
- **Template string**: A `t"..."` literal that produces a `string.templatelib.Template` object with inspectable static and dynamic parts.

Mini Quiz

1. **Which function definition safely handles an optional list of tags without risking shared mutable state across calls?**

   A. `def create(tags=[]): ...`

   B. `def create(tags={}): ...`

   C. `def create(tags=None): ...`

   D. `def create(tags=set()): ...`

2. **Given the signature** `def build_note_id(title: str, *, prefix: str = "note") -> str:`**, which call correctly supplies a custom prefix?**

   A. `build_note_id("Hello", "hw")`

   B. `build_note_id("Hello")`

   C. `build_note_id(title="Hello", "hw")`

   D. `build_note_id("Hello", prefix="hw")`

3. **In Python 3.14, what is the modern format-aware way to resolve deferred annotations at runtime?**

   A. Call `get_annotations(func, format=Format.VALUE)` from `annotationlib`

   B. Access `func.__annotations__.resolve()`

   C. Call `eval(func.__annotations__)`

   D. Call `func.get_annotations()`

4. **Consider a module constant** `LIMIT = 50` **and a function that defines** `LIMIT = 5` **locally, then calls** `process(LIMIT)`**. What value does** `process` **receive?**

   A. 50

   B. An `UnboundLocalError`

   C. `None`

   D. 5

5. **Which statement accurately describes a Python 3.14 template string (**`t"..."`**)?**

   A. It automatically escapes HTML in interpolations.

   B. It returns a plain `str` like an f-string.

C. It returns a `string.templatelib.Template` with inspectable interpolations.

D. It evaluates interpolations using implicit `str.format`.

Answers are provided in the Answer Key at the end of the book.

Activity

Extend the Personal Knowledge Tracker CLI with batch note creation and safe plaintext rendering.

- Open `src/knowledge_tracker/ch04_functions.py` in your editor.
- Add a function `batch_create_notes` that accepts `entries: list[dict[str, object]]` and returns `list[NoteDict]`. Iterate over `entries`, extract `title` and `body` as strings, and pass them to `safe_create_note`. Use `.get("tags")` to forward any tags; do not use a mutable default for the `entries` parameter.
- Validate tag values before passing them to `safe_create_note`: ensure the tags value is a list, keep only string elements, and convert each valid string to lowercase. Unchecked tag lists containing integers or None values will propagate errors downstream.
- Make `batch_create_notes` accept a keyword-only argument `*, strict: bool = False`. When `strict` is `True`, skip any entry where `title` or `body` is missing, empty, or whitespace-only, and return only the successfully created notes. When `strict` is `False`, attempt to create a note for every entry without pre-filtering, letting `safe_create_note` handle validation.
- Add a function `render_note_plaintext(note: NoteDict) -> str` that builds a t-string in the form `Title: {title}\nBody: {body}\nTags: {tag_str}` and passes it to `render_safe_html`. This reuses the escaping pipeline even for plain-text output.
- Extend `run_functions_demo()` to exercise both new functions, or place the demonstration code inside the existing `if __name__ == "__main__":` guard. The demo should call `get_annotations` with `format=Format.VALUE` on both new functions and print the resolved annotation dictionaries.
- Run the file with `uv run python -m knowledge_tracker.ch04_functions` and confirm that the batch function respects `strict`, the plaintext renderer escapes angle brackets, and the annotation inspection prints resolved types.

Chapter 5: Collections, Iteration, and Comprehensions

What You Will Learn

- Choose appropriate built-in collection types for note data
- Write list, dict, and set comprehensions to transform note collections concisely
- Implement generator functions to stream search results without loading full lists into memory
- Slice and sort note lists to implement recency views and pagination
- Apply the iterator protocol to consume note streams lazily

Prerequisites

- Completion of Chapter 2 (Values, Expressions, Strings, and Types) for `NoteDict` structure and basic note creation
- Completion of Chapter 3 (Control Flow and CLI Routing) for truthiness, filtering, and validation logic
- Completion of Chapter 4 (Functions, Scope, and Deferred Annotations) for function definitions, type hints, and keyword-only arguments

Concept Overview

Python provides four built-in collection types that cover most in-memory data shapes. Lists hold ordered sequences. Dictionaries map keys to values. Sets store unique hashable items. Tuples provide immutable sequences. For the Personal Knowledge Tracker CLI, these types are sufficient to organize notes, deduplicate tags, build lookup indexes, and present sorted views.

Comprehensions offer a declarative syntax for deriving one collection from another. List comprehensions transform and filter sequences in one expression. Dict and set comprehensions apply the same idea to mappings and unique collections. They are more concise than explicit loops and typically faster because the interpreter optimizes the single-expression iteration internally.

Eager materialization builds an entire result collection in memory immediately. Lazy evaluation produces values one at a time as the caller requests them. When you search a large note collection, building a full result list wastes memory if the caller only needs the first few matches. Generator expressions and generator functions solve this by yielding items lazily. The iterator protocol governs this behavior; every generator is an iterator, and every iterator exposes `__next__` through the built-in `next()` function.

This chapter expands the tracker from a flat in-memory list into a queryable collection. You will deduplicate tags, sort notes by creation time, index notes by tag for fast lookup, and stream search results without allocating intermediate lists. These patterns are the foundation for the file persistence layer you will add in Chapter 6.

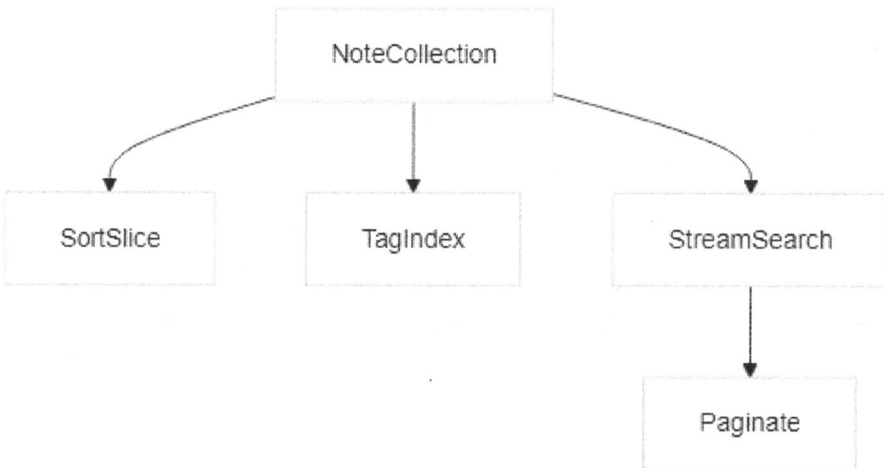

Step-by-Step Implementation

Step 1: Type Alias and Basic Collection Operations

This chapter continues using `NoteDict`, the dictionary type alias introduced in Chapter 2, along with the validation helpers `is_valid_note` and `note_has_tag` from Chapter 3. Start by importing them and giving the note list a meaningful type alias.

```
from knowledge_tracker.ch02_values import NoteDict
from knowledge_tracker.ch03_control_flow import is_valid_note,
note_has_tag

type NoteCollection = list[NoteDict]
```

Tuples provide immutable sequences. The function below partitions notes into valid and invalid groups, then returns them as a tuple.

```
def partition_notes(notes: NoteCollection) -> tuple[list[NoteDict],
list[NoteDict]]:
    valid = [n for n in notes if is_valid_note(n)]
    invalid = [n for n in notes if not is_valid_note(n)]
    return valid, invalid
```

Callers unpack the tuple into two distinct names.

```
valid_notes, invalid_notes = partition_notes(notes)
print(f"Valid: {len(valid_notes)}, Invalid: {len(invalid_notes)}")
```

A set comprehension is the most direct way to collect every unique tag across all notes. The equivalent nested loop makes the logic explicit.

```
def collect_unique_tags_loop(notes: NoteCollection) -> set[str]:
    tags: set[str] = set()
    for note in notes:
        note_tags = note.get("tags")
        if isinstance(note_tags, list):
            for tag in note_tags:
                if isinstance(tag, str) and tag.strip():
                    tags.add(tag.strip().lower())
    return tags
```

The comprehension collapses the same logic into one expression. It strips whitespace, lowercases each tag, and skips empty strings. The expression iterates over notes, then over each note's tag list, and emits a lowercased string only if the tag is actually a string and not empty.

```
def collect_unique_tags(notes: NoteCollection) -> set[str]:
    return {
        tag.strip().lower()
        for note in notes
        if isinstance(note.get("tags"), list)
        for tag in note["tags"]
```

```
        if isinstance(tag, str) and tag.strip()
    }
```

Nested comprehensions read from left to right like nested `for` loops. The outer loop processes notes; the inner loop processes tags. The resulting set automatically discards duplicates.

List and dict comprehensions follow the same pattern. `list_all_titles` filters invalid notes and extracts titles. `get_id_title_pairs` builds a mapping from note ID to title, validating that the ID is a string.

```
def list_all_titles(notes: NoteCollection) -> list[str]:
    return [note.get("title", "") for note in notes if
is_valid_note(note)]

def get_id_title_pairs(notes: NoteCollection) -> dict[str, str]:
    return {
        note["id"]: note.get("title", "")
        for note in notes
        if isinstance(note.get("id"), str) and is_valid_note(note)
    }
```

These functions are eager. They consume the entire input list and produce a new collection in memory. For the tracker's typical workload, that is exactly what you want for small derived views.

Step 2: Sorting and Slicing Sequences

Notes carry a `created` timestamp set by `safe_create_note` in Chapter 4. Because the value is a UTC ISO 8601 string with fixed-width fields (`YYYY-MM-DDTHH:MM:SS...`), lexicographic string ordering matches chronological ordering from oldest to newest. No parsing is required.

```
def sort_notes_by_created(notes: NoteCollection) -> list[NoteDict]:
    def _created_key(note: NoteDict) -> str:
        created = note.get("created", "")
        return created if isinstance(created, str) else ""
    return sorted(notes, key=_created_key, reverse=True)
```

The `sorted` built-in returns a new list. It leaves the original untouched. If you need to sort in place, call `.sort()` on the list; that method returns `None`. Prefer `sorted` unless you have a specific reason to mutate the source list.

Slicing extracts a prefix without copying the underlying note dictionaries. The slice `[:count]` returns up to `count` items and silently produces a shorter list if the source is smaller.

```
def get_recent_slice(notes: NoteCollection, count: int = 5) ->
list[NoteDict]:
    if count <= 0:
        return []
    return sort_notes_by_created(notes)[:count]
```

This function composes two operations: sort descending, then slice. The result is a lightweight view of the most recent notes.

Step 3: Indexing and Aggregation with Comprehensions

A dict comprehension can map each tag to the list of notes that contain it. The tracker uses this index to answer "show me every note tagged python" without scanning the full collection on each query.

```
def build_tag_index(notes: NoteCollection) -> dict[str,
list[NoteDict]]:
    return {
        tag: [n for n in notes if is_valid_note(n) and
note_has_tag(n, tag)]
        for tag in collect_unique_tags(notes)
    }
```

This is concise but not free. It iterates over every unique tag and scans the full note list for each one. For the tracker's typical scale, the clarity is worth the cost. If you index millions of notes, a single-pass loop with `dict.setdefault` is the better algorithm.

Counting tags is an aggregation, not a one-to-one mapping. The standard library's `Counter` class is purpose-built for this task. Feeding it a generator expression keeps the intermediate footprint small.

```
from collections import Counter

def count_tags(notes: NoteCollection) -> dict[str, int]:
    return dict(Counter(
        tag.strip().lower()
        for note in notes
        if is_valid_note(note) and isinstance(note.get("tags"), list)
        for tag in note["tags"]
```

```
        if isinstance(tag, str) and tag.strip()
    ))
```

`Counter` is a dict subclass, so the return type annotation remains honest. Converting it back to `dict` makes the contract explicit for callers that do not need counting-specific methods.

Step 4: Streaming Search with Generators

Generators implement the iterator protocol. Each generator object exposes a `__next__` method that the built-in `next()` function calls to retrieve the next value. Execution pauses at `yield` and resumes on the next call. Generator functions use the `yield` statement to produce a sequence of values lazily. When a generator function is called, it returns an iterator object immediately. No code inside the function body runs until the caller requests the first value with `next()`.

```
from collections.abc import Iterator

def stream_search_results(
    notes: NoteCollection,
    query: str,
) -> Iterator[NoteDict]:
    lowered = query.lower()
    for note in notes:
        if not is_valid_note(note):
            continue
        title = note.get("title", "")
        body = note.get("body", "")
        raw_source = note.get("source_url")
        source = raw_source.lower() if isinstance(raw_source, str)
else ""
        if (
            lowered in title.lower()
            or lowered in body.lower()
            or lowered in source.lower()
        ):
            yield note
```

Each `yield` pauses execution and saves the function's local state. The next time the caller advances the iterator, execution resumes immediately after the `yield`. This means the tracker can search thousands of notes but only materializes one `NoteDict` at a time. I once debugged a CLI search that crashed from a list comprehension materializing ten thousand notes no one scrolled past.

You can compose generators by calling one generator function inside another.

```
def stream_previews(
    notes: NoteCollection,
    query: str,
) -> Iterator[str]:
    for note in stream_search_results(notes, query):
        yield preview_note(note)
```

`stream_previews` delegates filtering to `stream_search_results` and transforms each match into a preview string. The caller sees a single uniform stream even though two generators cooperate under the hood.

Step 5: Pagination and the Iterator Protocol

Before building pagination, it helps to see the iterator protocol directly. Calling `iter()` on a list returns an iterator object. Calling `next()` on that object returns the next item. When the sequence ends, `next()` raises `StopIteration` unless you provide a default.

```
def peek_first_title(notes: NoteCollection) -> str | None:
    it = iter(notes)
    first = next(it, None)
    if first is None:
        return None
    return first.get("title", "")
```

Pagination splits a flat sequence into fixed-size chunks. Instead of returning one giant list, a generator yields pages as smaller lists.

```
def paginate_notes(
    notes: NoteCollection,
    page_size: int,
) -> Iterator[list[NoteDict]]:
    if page_size <= 0:
        raise ValueError("page_size must be positive")
    iterator = iter(notes)
    while True:
        page = []
        for _ in range(page_size):
            try:
                page.append(next(iterator))
```

```
            except StopIteration:
                if page:
                    yield page
                return
        yield page
```

This function demonstrates the iterator protocol explicitly. `iter(notes)` asks the list for an iterator object. `next(iterator)` advances that object by one position. When the iterator is exhausted, it raises `StopIteration`, which the `for` loop normally catches automatically. Here we catch it manually to flush the final partial page.

The built-in `next()` accepts a default value. This avoids wrapping every lookup in a `try` block.

```
def find_first_by_tag(
    notes: NoteCollection,
    tag: str,
) -> NoteDict | None:
    return next(
        (note for note in notes if note_has_tag(note, tag)),
        None,
    )
```

The first argument is a generator expression; the second is the fallback. If no note matches, the function returns `None` instead of raising `StopIteration`.

Import `safe_create_note` from Chapter 4 before running the demonstration.

```
from knowledge_tracker.ch04_functions import safe_create_note
```

The demonstration script creates three sample notes and exercises every function introduced in this chapter.

```
def demo_ch05() -> None:
    notes: NoteCollection = [
        safe_create_note(
            title="Python 3.14 Template Strings",
            body="t-strings enable safe interpolation inspection.",
            tags=["python", "templates", "security"],
        ),
        safe_create_note(
            title="Async I/O Patterns",
            body="Use asyncio.TaskGroup for structured concurrency.",
            tags=["python", "async", "patterns"],
```

```
        ),
        safe_create_note(
            title="Zstandard Compression",
            body="compression.zstd ships in the standard library.",
            tags=["python", "compression", "stdlib"],
        ),
    ]

    valid, invalid = partition_notes(notes)
    print(f"Valid: {len(valid)}, Invalid: {len(invalid)}")

    print("Unique tags:", collect_unique_tags(notes))
    print("Titles:", list_all_titles(notes))
    print("ID pairs:", get_id_title_pairs(notes))

    recent = get_recent_slice(notes, count=2)
    print("Recent count:", len(recent))

    index = build_tag_index(notes)
    print("Notes tagged 'python':", len(index.get("python", [])))

    counts = count_tags(notes)
    print("Tag counts:", counts)

    print("Search stream:")
    for preview in stream_previews(notes, "python"):
        print(" ", preview)

    print("Pages:")
    for page in paginate_notes(notes, page_size=2):
        print("  page len:", len(page))

    first = find_first_by_tag(notes, "async")
    print("First async note:", first.get("title") if first else
"None")

    print("Peek first:", peek_first_title(notes))

if __name__ == "__main__":
    demo_ch05()
```

The demonstration exercises every function introduced in this chapter. Eager functions like `collect_unique_tags` and `build_tag_index` materialize complete collections for immediate inspection. Lazy generators like `stream_previews` and `paginate_notes` yield items only as the `for` loop requests them. This composition lets the CLI layer consume search results page by page without holding the entire result set in memory.

Run the module with `uv run python -m knowledge_tracker.ch05_collections`.

Full Example

The consolidated module below mixes eager comprehensions for small derived data with generators for open-ended search and pagination. It depends on `NoteDict` and `preview_note` from Chapter 2, `is_valid_note` and `note_has_tag` from Chapter 3, and `safe_create_note` from Chapter 4.

```
# src/knowledge_tracker/ch05_collections.py
from collections import Counter
from collections.abc import Iterator

from knowledge_tracker.ch02_values import NoteDict, preview_note
from knowledge_tracker.ch03_control_flow import is_valid_note,
note_has_tag
from knowledge_tracker.ch04_functions import safe_create_note

type NoteCollection = list[NoteDict]

def partition_notes(notes: NoteCollection) -> tuple[list[NoteDict],
list[NoteDict]]:
    valid = [n for n in notes if is_valid_note(n)]
    invalid = [n for n in notes if not is_valid_note(n)]
    return valid, invalid

def collect_unique_tags_loop(notes: NoteCollection) -> set[str]:
    tags: set[str] = set()
    for note in notes:
        note_tags = note.get("tags")
        if isinstance(note_tags, list):
            for tag in note_tags:
                if isinstance(tag, str) and tag.strip():
                    tags.add(tag.strip().lower())
    return tags

def collect_unique_tags(notes: NoteCollection) -> set[str]:
    return {
        tag.strip().lower()
        for note in notes
        if isinstance(note.get("tags"), list)
        for tag in note["tags"]
        if isinstance(tag, str) and tag.strip()
    }

def list_all_titles(notes: NoteCollection) -> list[str]:
    return [note.get("title", "") for note in notes if
is_valid_note(note)]

def get_id_title_pairs(notes: NoteCollection) -> dict[str, str]:
    return {
        note["id"]: note.get("title", "")
        for note in notes
        if isinstance(note.get("id"), str) and is_valid_note(note)
```

```
    }

def sort_notes_by_created(notes: NoteCollection) -> list[NoteDict]:
    def _created_key(note: NoteDict) -> str:
        created = note.get("created", "")
        return created if isinstance(created, str) else ""
    return sorted(notes, key=_created_key, reverse=True)

def get_recent_slice(notes: NoteCollection, count: int = 5) ->
list[NoteDict]:
    if count <= 0:
        return []
    return sort_notes_by_created(notes)[:count]

def build_tag_index(notes: NoteCollection) -> dict[str,
list[NoteDict]]:
    return {
        tag: [n for n in notes if is_valid_note(n) and
note_has_tag(n, tag)]
        for tag in collect_unique_tags(notes)
    }

def count_tags(notes: NoteCollection) -> dict[str, int]:
    return dict(Counter(
        tag.strip().lower()
        for note in notes
        if is_valid_note(note) and isinstance(note.get("tags"), list)
        for tag in note["tags"]
        if isinstance(tag, str) and tag.strip()
    ))

def stream_search_results(
    notes: NoteCollection,
    query: str,
) -> Iterator[NoteDict]:
    lowered = query.lower()
    for note in notes:
        if not is_valid_note(note):
            continue
        title = note.get("title", "")
        body = note.get("body", "")
        raw_source = note.get("source_url")
        source = raw_source.lower() if isinstance(raw_source, str)
else ""
        if (
            lowered in title.lower()
            or lowered in body.lower()
            or lowered in source.lower()
        ):
            yield note

def stream_previews(
    notes: NoteCollection,
    query: str,
```

```
) -> Iterator[str]:
    for note in stream_search_results(notes, query):
        yield preview_note(note)

def peek_first_title(notes: NoteCollection) -> str | None:
    it = iter(notes)
    first = next(it, None)
    if first is None:
        return None
    return first.get("title", "")

def paginate_notes(
    notes: NoteCollection,
    page_size: int,
) -> Iterator[list[NoteDict]]:
    if page_size <= 0:
        raise ValueError("page_size must be positive")
    iterator = iter(notes)
    while True:
        page = []
        for _ in range(page_size):
            try:
                page.append(next(iterator))
            except StopIteration:
                if page:
                    yield page
                return
        yield page

def find_first_by_tag(
    notes: NoteCollection,
    tag: str,
) -> NoteDict | None:
    return next(
        (note for note in notes if note_has_tag(note, tag)),
        None,
    )

def demo_ch05() -> None:
    notes: NoteCollection = [
        safe_create_note(
            title="Python 3.14 Template Strings",
            body="t-strings enable safe interpolation inspection.",
            tags=["python", "templates", "security"],
        ),
        safe_create_note(
            title="Async I/O Patterns",
            body="Use asyncio.TaskGroup for structured concurrency.",
            tags=["python", "async", "patterns"],
        ),
        safe_create_note(
            title="Zstandard Compression",
            body="compression.zstd ships in the standard library.",
            tags=["python", "compression", "stdlib"],
```

```
        ),
    ]

    valid, invalid = partition_notes(notes)
    print(f"Valid: {len(valid)}, Invalid: {len(invalid)}")

    print("Unique tags:", collect_unique_tags(notes))
    print("Titles:", list_all_titles(notes))
    print("ID pairs:", get_id_title_pairs(notes))

    recent = get_recent_slice(notes, count=2)
    print("Recent count:", len(recent))

    index = build_tag_index(notes)
    print("Notes tagged 'python':", len(index.get("python", [])))

    counts = count_tags(notes)
    print("Tag counts:", counts)

    print("Search stream:")
    for preview in stream_previews(notes, "python"):
        print(" ", preview)

    print("Pages:")
    for page in paginate_notes(notes, page_size=2):
        print("  page len:", len(page))

    first = find_first_by_tag(notes, "async")
    print("First async note:", first.get("title") if first else
"None")

    print("Peek first:", peek_first_title(notes))

if __name__ == "__main__":
    demo_ch05()
```

The module keeps all collection operations in one place. Eager functions like `collect_unique_tags` and `build_tag_index` produce concrete data structures for immediate use. Lazy functions like `stream_search_results` and `paginate_notes` return iterators that the caller drives with a `for` loop or `next()`. This separation of concerns makes it easy to swap an in-memory list for a database cursor later without rewriting the CLI layer.

Common Mistakes

- Mutating a list while iterating over it. Removing items from a list inside a `for` loop over that list skips elements or raises errors. Build a new list with a comprehension, or iterate over a copy.

- Using a list comprehension for side effects. `[print(n) for n in notes]` builds a list of `None` values and wastes memory. Use a plain `for` loop when you do not need the resulting collection.
- Treating a generator like a list. Generators support iteration only once. Calling `len()` or indexing with `[0]` raises `TypeError`. Convert to a list explicitly if you need random access.
- Confusing `sorted` with `list.sort`. `sorted` returns a new list. `list.sort` sorts in place and returns `None`. Assigning the result of `.sort()` to a variable silently binds `None`.
- Letting `StopIteration` leak from a generator. Manually calling `next()` without a default value raises `StopIteration`. In most contexts Python handles this for you, but inside a generator or complex control flow it can mask bugs. Always provide a default to `next()` when a missing value is expected.
- Slicing with unchecked negative page sizes. Passing a negative count to a slice like `[:count]` does not raise an error; it produces unexpected results. Validate bounds before slicing.

Never mutate a list while iterating over it.

Performance and Production Considerations

Eager comprehensions materialize entire collections in memory. A list comprehension that filters ten thousand notes creates a new list of ten thousand references. For small working sets, this is fast and simple. For large collections, generator functions avoid materializing an intermediate full result list. The source collection still resides in memory, but each yielded item is processed and discarded individually.

The `build_tag_index` dict comprehension is O(n * m) where m is the number of unique tags. A single-pass loop with `setdefault` scales linearly with the total tag count. Avoid nested comprehensions over large collections; prefer a plain loop when algorithmic complexity matters.

Generators are single-use. Once you exhaust an iterator, it will not restart.

If you need to iterate the same data multiple times, either build a list or recreate the generator.

For the `created` field, lexicographic ordering is safe only while timestamps remain uniform and UTC-based.

If timestamps mix timezones or formats, the sort order becomes unpredictable. Keep timestamps uniform and UTC-based, as `safe_create_note` does.

`paginate_notes` yields chunks that share references to the original note dictionaries. Modifying a note inside a page mutates the source collection.

Deep-copy each note before appending it to the chunk if you need immutable pages.

Summary

You expanded the Personal Knowledge Tracker CLI from a flat list into a rich, queryable collection. You used list, dict, and set comprehensions to transform notes into titles, ID pairs, tag indexes, and unique tag sets. You sorted and sliced sequences to produce recency views without mutating source data. Generator functions and the iterator protocol let you stream search results and paginate notes lazily, keeping memory usage low even as the collection grows.

These patterns are the foundation for the next step. In Chapter 6, you will persist notes to disk with JSON, compress exports with `compression.zstd`, and handle the file errors that inevitably appear when a CLI touches the filesystem.

Key Terms

- **List comprehension**: A declarative expression that filters and transforms an iterable into a new list in a single line.
- **Dict comprehension**: An expression that constructs a dictionary by iterating over a source and defining key-value pairs.
- **Set comprehension**: An expression that builds a set of unique values from an iterable, automatically discarding duplicates.
- **Generator function**: A function containing `yield` that returns an iterator and produces values lazily, one at a time.
- **Iterator protocol**: The contract requiring `__iter__` and `__next__` methods, enabling sequential consumption with `for` or `next()`.

- **Slice**: An index notation such as `[:count]` that extracts a subsequence without mutating the original collection.

Mini Quiz

1. **What is the primary advantage of using a list comprehension over an explicit `for` loop to build a list of note titles?**

   A. It evaluates the iteration more efficiently than an explicit `for` loop, often improving performance

   B. It automatically validates note data using `is_valid_note`

   C. It allows mutation of the source list during iteration

   D. It returns a generator instead of a list

2. **Given the following generator function:**

```
def stream_notes(notes):
    for note in notes:
        if note.get("title"):
            yield note
```

Which statement accurately describes `results = stream_notes(my_notes)`?

   A. It immediately builds a list of all matching notes and assigns it to `results`

   B. It executes the loop until the first `yield`, then assigns the note to `results`

   C. It raises `StopIteration` because the generator is empty until `next()` is called

   D. It returns a generator object that will lazily produce matches when iterated

3. **The Personal Knowledge Tracker holds 100,000 notes in memory. Which approach minimizes memory usage when searching for a keyword and displaying only the first 10 matches?**

   A. Use a generator function that yields matches and break after 10 iterations

   B. Build a list comprehension of all matches, then slice the first 10

   C. Sort the full note list with `sorted()`, then scan linearly

   D. Build a dict mapping every tag to its notes before searching

4. **What does the expression `next(iterator, None)` evaluate to when `iterator` has no remaining items?**

   A. It raises `StopIteration`

   B. It returns `None`

   C. It restarts the iterator from the beginning

   D. It raises `ValueError`

5. **Which statement about Python's `sorted()` built-in is true?**

   A. It sorts the original list in place and returns `None`

   B. It returns a new sorted list and leaves the original unchanged

   C. It accepts only lists of strings

   D. It modifies the `key` function during iteration

Answers are provided in the Answer Key at the end of the book.

Activity

Extend the Personal Knowledge Tracker CLI with a tag cloud and a paginated recency view.

- Add a generator function `stream_notes_by_tag(notes, tag)` to `ch05_collections.py` that lazily yields notes matching a given tag using `note_has_tag`. Include a `print` call inside the generator that outputs each note ID as it is yielded. Then iterate with a `for` loop and break after two results; verify in the console output that only two IDs were printed, confirming that lazy processing stopped early and not all notes were evaluated.
- Implement `get_tag_cloud(notes) -> dict[str, int]` using `collections.Counter` and a generator expression that lowercases tags. Print the cloud in the demo to verify counts.
- Compose `sort_notes_by_created` and `paginate_notes` into a new function `get_recent_paginated(notes, page_size, max_pages=None)`. After sorting, pass the result to `paginate_notes`. If `max_pages` is provided, stop yielding after that many pages.
- Update `demo_ch05` to create at least five notes with overlapping tags. Display the tag cloud, stream two notes for a specific tag, and print the first two pages of recent notes.
- Run the module with `uv run python -m knowledge_tracker.ch05_collections` and confirm that pagination respects `max_pages` and that streaming search does not materialize the full result set.

Chapter 6: Files, Paths, I/O, and Basic File Errors

What You Will Learn

- Use `pathlib.Path` for cross-platform filesystem operations in the Personal Knowledge Tracker CLI
- Persist note collections to JSON using context managers and explicit UTF-8 encoding
- Load note collections safely, returning empty defaults when files are missing or corrupt
- Export note collections to Zstandard-compressed archives with Python 3.14's `compression.zstd`
- Integrate file I/O into the CLI so note data survives process restarts
- Isolate file-related failures from domain logic using structured exception handling

Prerequisites

- Completion of Chapter 2 (Values, Expressions, Strings, and Types) for `NoteDict` structure and the `create_note` / `preview_note` helpers
- Completion of Chapter 3 (Control Flow and CLI Routing) for `argparse` subcommands, `is_valid_note`, `summarize_notes`, and `run_search`
- Completion of Chapter 4 (Functions, Scope, and Deferred Annotations) for `safe_create_note` and keyword-only argument patterns
- Completion of Chapter 5 (Collections, Iteration, and Comprehensions) for list and dictionary operations

Concept Overview

Until now, the Personal Knowledge Tracker CLI has stored every note in memory. The collection vanishes on process exit. This chapter introduces local file persistence so the tracker remembers state across restarts.

Python represents filesystem paths with `pathlib.Path`. Unlike string manipulation, `Path` objects expose methods such as `mkdir`, `read_text`, and `write_bytes`. They translate automatically between Windows backslashes and POSIX forward slashes. Cross-platform path bugs disappear.

Files are external resources. The `with` statement implements context managers that guarantee file handles close even when exceptions interrupt processing. Deterministic cleanup is safer than manual `close` calls.

The standard library's `json` module serializes Python lists and dictionaries to text. Pass `encoding="utf-8"` to preserve emoji and international characters. On Windows, omitting the encoding invites legacy code pages that mangle text.

I/O is inherently unreliable. Users delete files, disks fill up, and power failures leave half-written data. Catching `FileNotFoundError` and `json.JSONDecodeError` on load lets the application start with an empty collection. Write and export operations propagate `OSError` to the caller. CLI handlers catch these and report the failure without crashing.

Python 3.14 adds `compression.zstd` to the standard library. Zstandard offers better compression ratios and faster speeds than `gzip` for many workloads. The tracker uses it for compressed exports.

This chapter keeps file path resolution, serialization format, and domain logic in separate functions. That separation makes it trivial to replace JSON with a database later. Chapter 8 will build on this boundary.

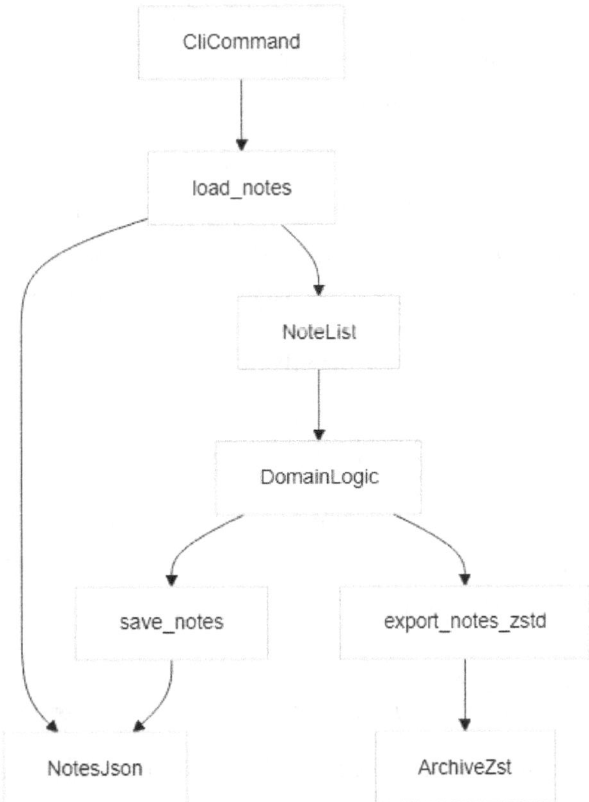

Step-by-Step Implementation

Step 1: Resolve the Tracker Data Directory and Note File Path

Every persisted application needs a stable location on disk. The following functions resolve a hidden directory under the user's home folder and ensure it exists before any write occurs.

```
from pathlib import Path

def get_data_dir() -> Path:
    return Path.home() / ".knowledge_tracker"

def get_notes_file(data_dir: Path | None = None) -> Path:
    if data_dir is None:
        data_dir = get_data_dir()
    data_dir.mkdir(parents=True, exist_ok=True)
    return data_dir / "notes.json"
```

`Path.home()` returns the user's home directory on any platform. A hidden directory under the home folder keeps tracker data out of the working tree and follows the convention for user-specific application data. The `/` operator joins path segments using the correct separator.

`mkdir(parents=True, exist_ok=True)` creates missing parent directories silently. The call is idempotent. Running it once or many times produces the same result, and `exist_ok=True` prevents race-condition crashes if another process creates the directory between the existence check and the creation.

Directory creation races are common.

Step 2: Save Notes to JSON

The save function serializes the in-memory note list to a JSON file. It uses a context manager so the file handle closes automatically, and it explicitly declares UTF-8 encoding.

```
import json
from knowledge_tracker.ch02_values import NoteDict

def save_notes(notes: list[NoteDict], path: Path | None = None) ->
None:
    if path is None:
```

```
    path = get_notes_file()
with path.open("w", encoding="utf-8") as handle:
    json.dump(notes, handle, indent=2, ensure_ascii=False)
```

Always pass `encoding="utf-8"` to `open()`. Platform defaults are a liability.

`json.dump` writes the list directly to the file object. The `indent=2` argument produces human-readable output, which is valuable for debugging. `ensure_ascii=False` lets Unicode characters pass through unescaped. The `"w"` mode opens the file for text writing. Compressed archives require `"wb"`.

Step 3: Load Notes Safely

Loading must tolerate missing files and corruption. A first run has no data file yet. A crash during a previous write can leave invalid JSON. The loader catches these specific exceptions and returns an empty list.

```
def load_notes(path: Path | None = None) -> list[NoteDict]:
    if path is None:
        path = get_notes_file()
    try:
        with path.open("r", encoding="utf-8") as handle:
            data = json.load(handle)
    except FileNotFoundError:
        return []
    except json.JSONDecodeError:
        return []
    if not isinstance(data, list):
        return []
    return [item for item in data if isinstance(item, dict)]
```

Don't use bare `except` clauses; they hide bugs. Catch specific exceptions only.

The function also guards against a top-level JSON object or scalar by checking `isinstance(data, list)`. The list comprehension filters out any non-dictionary items that external tools may have inserted. Deeper structural validation, such as checking required fields, remains the responsibility of downstream domain functions like `is_valid_note`. This defensive filter prevents runtime type errors without duplicating validation logic.

A hand-edited notes file once crashed my tracker. A bare string had leaked into the JSON array, and the `isinstance(item, dict)` guard would have prevented that failure.

Step 4: Export Notes to Zstandard

Python 3.14 includes `compression.zstd` for standard-library Zstandard compression. The export function serializes notes to JSON bytes, compresses them, and writes the result to disk in binary mode.

```
from compression.zstd import compress

def export_notes_zstd(notes: list[NoteDict], archive_path: Path) ->
None:
    archive_path.parent.mkdir(parents=True, exist_ok=True)
    payload = json.dumps(notes, indent=2,
ensure_ascii=False).encode("utf-8")
    compressed = compress(payload)
    with archive_path.open("wb") as handle:
        handle.write(compressed)
```

`archive_path.parent.mkdir(parents=True, exist_ok=True)` ensures the destination directory exists before writing. Notice the `"wb"` mode. `json.dumps` returns a string, which `.encode("utf-8")` converts to bytes. Compression produces bytes, not text, so writing them in text mode raises `TypeError`. The one-shot `compress` function returns a complete Zstandard frame in a single call, which is the right fit for serializing one archive at once.

Step 5: Integrate Persistence into the CLI

The final step wires file I/O into the Personal Knowledge Tracker CLI. Each command handler loads the current collection from disk, performs its work, and persists changes when appropriate. The data directory becomes the single source of truth.

```
import argparse
from pathlib import Path

from knowledge_tracker.ch02_values import preview_note
from knowledge_tracker.ch03_control_flow import is_valid_note,
run_search, summarize_notes
from knowledge_tracker.ch04_functions import safe_create_note

def build_persisted_parser() -> argparse.ArgumentParser:
    parser = argparse.ArgumentParser(prog="knowledge-tracker")
    subparsers = parser.add_subparsers(dest="command", required=True)

    create = subparsers.add_parser("create")
    create.add_argument("--title", required=True)
    create.add_argument("--body", required=True)
```

```
    create.add_argument("--tag", action="append", default=[])
    create.add_argument("--source-url", default=None)

    list_cmd = subparsers.add_parser("list")
    list_cmd.add_argument("--limit", type=int, default=None)

    search = subparsers.add_parser("search")
    search.add_argument("query")
    search.add_argument("--tag", action="append", default=[])

    export = subparsers.add_parser("export")
    export.add_argument("--output", default=None)

    return parser

def run_create_persisted(args: argparse.Namespace) -> str:
    notes = load_notes()
    title = args.title.strip()
    body = args.body.strip()
    if not title or not body:
        return "Error: title and body cannot be empty."
    note = safe_create_note(
        title=title,
        body=body,
        tags=args.tag,
        source_url=args.source_url,
    )
    if not is_valid_note(note):
        return "Error: validation failed."
    notes.append(note)
    try:
        save_notes(notes)
    except OSError as e:
        return f"Error: failed to save notes ({e})"
    return f"Created note: {preview_note(note)}"

def run_list_persisted(args: argparse.Namespace) -> str:
    notes = load_notes()
    if args.limit is not None and args.limit <= 0:
        return "Error: limit must be a positive integer."
    return summarize_notes(notes, limit=args.limit)

def run_search_persisted(args: argparse.Namespace) -> str:
    notes = load_notes()
    return run_search(notes, args)

def run_export_persisted(args: argparse.Namespace) -> str:
    notes = load_notes()
    if args.output:
        archive_path = Path(args.output)
    else:
        archive_path = get_notes_file().with_suffix(".json.zst")
    try:
        export_notes_zstd(notes, archive_path)
```

```
    except OSError as e:
        return f"Error: failed to export archive ({e})"
    return f"Exported {len(notes)} notes to {archive_path}"

def run_persisted_cli() -> None:
    parser = build_persisted_parser()
    args = parser.parse_args()
    if args.command == "create":
        result = run_create_persisted(args)
    elif args.command == "list":
        result = run_list_persisted(args)
    elif args.command == "search":
        result = run_search_persisted(args)
    elif args.command == "export":
        result = run_export_persisted(args)
    else:
        result = "Unknown command"
    print(result)
```

Load data inside each command handler. Global state in CLI tools causes stale data and race conditions.

Each handler calls `load_notes` at the start of its execution. Every CLI invocation is a separate process, so the handler always sees the latest disk state. `run_create_persisted` appends the new note and immediately calls `save_notes`, catching `OSError` to report disk failures gracefully. `run_export_persisted` resolves an archive path; if the user omits `--output`, it derives a filename next to the JSON store.

Separate processes eliminate stale data.

Run the module directly to verify persistence:

```
uv run python -m knowledge_tracker.ch06_io create --title
"Persistence" --body "Notes survive restarts." --tag python
uv run python -m knowledge_tracker.ch06_io list
uv run python -m knowledge_tracker.ch06_io search python
uv run python -m knowledge_tracker.ch06_io export --output
backup.json.zst
```

The first command creates a note and writes it to `~/.knowledge_tracker/notes.json`. The second loads that file and prints a preview. The third searches the persisted collection. The fourth produces a Zstandard-compressed archive.

Full Example

The following module, `ch06_io.py`, combines every function introduced in this chapter into a single runnable script. Copy it into the `src/knowledge_tracker/` package to add persistence to the tracker.

```
import argparse
import json
from pathlib import Path

from compression.zstd import compress

from knowledge_tracker.ch02_values import NoteDict, preview_note
from knowledge_tracker.ch03_control_flow import is_valid_note,
run_search, summarize_notes
from knowledge_tracker.ch04_functions import safe_create_note

def get_data_dir() -> Path:
    return Path.home() / ".knowledge_tracker"

def get_notes_file(data_dir: Path | None = None) -> Path:
    if data_dir is None:
        data_dir = get_data_dir()
    data_dir.mkdir(parents=True, exist_ok=True)
    return data_dir / "notes.json"

def save_notes(notes: list[NoteDict], path: Path | None = None) ->
None:
    if path is None:
        path = get_notes_file()
    with path.open("w", encoding="utf-8") as handle:
        json.dump(notes, handle, indent=2, ensure_ascii=False)

def load_notes(path: Path | None = None) -> list[NoteDict]:
    if path is None:
        path = get_notes_file()
    try:
        with path.open("r", encoding="utf-8") as handle:
            data = json.load(handle)
    except FileNotFoundError:
        return []
    except json.JSONDecodeError:
        return []
    if not isinstance(data, list):
        return []
    return [item for item in data if isinstance(item, dict)]

def export_notes_zstd(notes: list[NoteDict], archive_path: Path) ->
None:
    archive_path.parent.mkdir(parents=True, exist_ok=True)
    payload = json.dumps(notes, indent=2,
ensure_ascii=False).encode("utf-8")
```

```
    compressed = compress(payload)
    with archive_path.open("wb") as handle:
        handle.write(compressed)

def build_persisted_parser() -> argparse.ArgumentParser:
    parser = argparse.ArgumentParser(prog="knowledge-tracker")
    subparsers = parser.add_subparsers(dest="command", required=True)

    create = subparsers.add_parser("create")
    create.add_argument("--title", required=True)
    create.add_argument("--body", required=True)
    create.add_argument("--tag", action="append", default=[])
    create.add_argument("--source-url", default=None)

    list_cmd = subparsers.add_parser("list")
    list_cmd.add_argument("--limit", type=int, default=None)

    search = subparsers.add_parser("search")
    search.add_argument("query")
    search.add_argument("--tag", action="append", default=[])

    export = subparsers.add_parser("export")
    export.add_argument("--output", default=None)

    return parser

def run_create_persisted(args: argparse.Namespace) -> str:
    notes = load_notes()
    title = args.title.strip()
    body = args.body.strip()
    if not title or not body:
        return "Error: title and body cannot be empty."
    note = safe_create_note(
        title=title,
        body=body,
        tags=args.tag,
        source_url=args.source_url,
    )
    if not is_valid_note(note):
        return "Error: validation failed."
    notes.append(note)
    try:
        save_notes(notes)
    except OSError as e:
        return f"Error: failed to save notes ({e})"
    return f"Created note: {preview_note(note)}"

def run_list_persisted(args: argparse.Namespace) -> str:
    notes = load_notes()
    if args.limit is not None and args.limit <= 0:
        return "Error: limit must be a positive integer."
    return summarize_notes(notes, limit=args.limit)

def run_search_persisted(args: argparse.Namespace) -> str:
```

```
    notes = load_notes()
    return run_search(notes, args)

def run_export_persisted(args: argparse.Namespace) -> str:
    notes = load_notes()
    if args.output:
        archive_path = Path(args.output)
    else:
        archive_path = get_notes_file().with_suffix(".json.zst")
    try:
        export_notes_zstd(notes, archive_path)
    except OSError as e:
        return f"Error: failed to export archive ({e})"
    return f"Exported {len(notes)} notes to {archive_path}"

def run_persisted_cli() -> None:
    parser = build_persisted_parser()
    args = parser.parse_args()
    if args.command == "create":
        result = run_create_persisted(args)
    elif args.command == "list":
        result = run_list_persisted(args)
    elif args.command == "search":
        result = run_search_persisted(args)
    elif args.command == "export":
        result = run_export_persisted(args)
    else:
        result = "Unknown command"
    print(result)

if __name__ == "__main__":
    run_persisted_cli()
```

Run the script with the same commands shown in Step 5:

```
uv run python -m knowledge_tracker.ch06_io create --title "Full
Example" --body "All persistence wired." --tag demo
uv run python -m knowledge_tracker.ch06_io list
uv run python -m knowledge_tracker.ch06_io export
```

The module separates concerns cleanly. `get_data_dir` and `get_notes_file` own path resolution. `save_notes` and `load_notes` own JSON serialization. `export_notes_zstd` owns compression. The CLI handlers orchestrate these utilities without embedding filesystem details into domain logic. That boundary keeps the Chapter 8 refactor to a `NoteRepository` protocol clean.

Common Mistakes

- **Using string concatenation instead of `pathlib.Path`.** Manually concatenating paths with `+ "/"` or backslash literals invites slash-direction bugs on Windows. `os.path.join` avoids some of these issues but is less ergonomic than `pathlib`. Use `Path` objects and the `/` operator.
- **Omitting `encoding="utf-8"` when opening text files.** On Windows, the default encoding may be `cp1252`. This corrupts Unicode characters during save or load. Always specify UTF-8 for JSON and text configuration files.
- **Catching bare `Exception` around file I/O.** A bare `except` masks programming errors such as `TypeError` or `AttributeError`. Catch specific exceptions only.
- **Forgetting the `with` statement around file operations.** Calling `open`, then `write`, then `close` manually leaks file handles if an exception occurs between `open` and `close`. Context managers guarantee cleanup.
- **Writing compressed data in text mode.** `compression.zstd` produces bytes. Opening the archive with `"w"` instead of `"wb"` raises `TypeError` when writing. Use binary mode for all non-text payloads.
- **Mutating the loaded note list without calling `save_notes`.** Domain changes exist only in memory until persisted. After appending, deleting, or editing notes, invoke the save function or the changes disappear on process exit.

Performance and Production Considerations

JSON is human-readable but not space-efficient. For large collections, the Zstandard export reduces disk usage significantly while remaining fast to compress and decompress.

Loading the entire collection into memory suits the Personal Knowledge Tracker CLI because it is a single-user local tool. Do not use this pattern for multi-gigabyte datasets. Stream data or use a database instead.

`Path.mkdir(parents=True, exist_ok=True)` is idempotent and safe for concurrent process startup. Multiple CLI invocations survive even if the directory already exists.

The one-shot `compress` function defaults to compression level 3 and returns a complete frame in a single call, which is ideal for serializing one archive at a time. For streaming large payloads in chunks, `ZstdCompressor` supports incremental `.compress()` calls followed by a final `.flush()` to emit the frame tail; the tracker's single-archive exports do not need that complexity.

The current implementation rewrites the entire `notes.json` file on every create operation. This is O(n) with collection size. For frequent writes, append-only journals or SQLite are better fits. Chapter 8 will introduce structured storage that can mitigate this cost.

For production tools, use atomic writes: serialize to a temporary file in the same directory, then call `os.replace` to swap it into place. This prevents data loss if the process crashes during a write.

Explicit UTF-8 encoding avoids locale-dependent behavior on Windows servers and CI runners. Always set the encoding parameter.

Summary

This chapter added durable storage to the Personal Knowledge Tracker CLI. `pathlib.Path` provides cross-platform path resolution. Context managers guarantee that file handles close correctly. JSON with explicit UTF-8 encoding preserves the note collection in a human-readable format. Structured exception handling for `FileNotFoundError` and `json.JSONDecodeError` lets the application start cleanly even when data is missing or corrupt. Python 3.14's `compression.zstd` provides compressed exports without third-party dependencies.

The CLI now loads notes at startup, persists them after creation, and exports compressed archives on demand. File I/O concerns remain separate from domain logic. That separation creates a clean boundary for the repository refactor in Chapter 8.

Key Terms

- **pathlib.Path**: Object-oriented filesystem path representation that handles cross-platform path separators and file operations.

- **Context manager**: Protocol, typically invoked with `with`, that acquires and releases resources deterministically; file handles close automatically even when exceptions occur.
- **JSON**: JavaScript Object Notation; Python's `json` module serializes lists and dictionaries to text and back.
- **UTF-8**: Variable-width character encoding that preserves Unicode text; pass it explicitly to `open()` to avoid platform-specific defaults.
- **FileNotFoundError**: Exception raised when an operation references a path that does not exist.
- **JSONDecodeError**: Exception raised when `json.load` or `json.loads` encounters malformed JSON.
- **compression.zstd**: Python 3.14 standard-library module providing Zstandard compression and decompression.
- **Binary mode**: File open mode prefixed with `b`, such as `"wb"`, for reading or writing bytes rather than decoded text.

Mini Quiz

1. **Which file mode must be used when writing Zstandard-compressed output with `compression.zstd`?**

   A. `"w"`

   B. `"wb"`

   C. `"r"`

   D. `"wt"`

2. **What does the `load_notes` function return when the notes JSON file is missing?**

   A. It raises `FileNotFoundError`

   B. It returns `None`

   C. It returns an empty list

   D. It returns an empty dictionary

3. **Why is `encoding="utf-8"` explicitly passed to `open()` when saving tracker notes?**

   A. To enable compression

   B. To ensure Unicode characters round-trip correctly on all platforms

   C. To prevent the file from being executable

   D. To suppress `JSONDecodeError`

4. **Which exception type should be caught when a previous crash left invalid JSON on disk?**

   A. `ValueError`

   B. `TypeError`

   C. `json.JSONDecodeError`

   D. `PermissionError`

5. **What does `path.mkdir(parents=True, exist_ok=True)` accomplish?**

   A. It removes the directory tree

   B. It creates missing directories and parents silently, even if the path already exists

   C. It converts the path to an absolute string

D. It locks the directory for exclusive access

Answers are provided in the Answer Key at the end of the book.

Activity

- Add a `delete` subcommand that accepts `--id` and removes the matching note from the loaded collection. Save the updated list back to disk and return a confirmation message. Don't raise an error if the ID isn't found; return a clear message instead.
- Add a `--backup` flag to the `create` subcommand. When present, copy the current `notes.json` to `notes_<timestamp>.json` in the same data directory before writing the new note. You'll generate the timestamp with `datetime.datetime.now().strftime("%Y%m%dT%H%M%S")`, which avoids the colons that `isoformat` produces and would be invalid in Windows filenames.
- Create two notes with `uv run python -m knowledge_tracker.ch06_io create`, run the `export` command, then verify the resulting `.zst` file exists. Decompress it with `compression.zstd` and confirm the JSON payload contains your note titles.

Part III: Program Structure

Chapter 7: Modules, Packages, and Project Layout

What You Will Learn

- Restructure the monolithic Personal Knowledge Tracker CLI into a maintainable package
- Organize code under `src/knowledge_tracker/` with separate domain, persistence, command, and CLI layers
- Distinguish source layout from flat layout and configure `pyproject.toml` for package discovery
- Use absolute imports to wire internal modules without creating circular dependencies
- Control the public package interface with `__init__.py` and `__all__`
- Execute the installed package with `uv run python -m knowledge_tracker`

Prerequisites

- Completion of Chapter 1: project setup with `uv`, `src/` layout, and `pyproject.toml` basics
- Completion of Chapter 2: `NoteDict` shape and note creation
- Completion of Chapter 3: `argparse` subparsers, `is_valid_note`, `filter_by_tag`, `summarize_notes`
- Completion of Chapter 4: function signatures and deferred annotations
- Completion of Chapter 5: collection operations
- Completion of Chapter 6: `pathlib`, JSON persistence, `save_notes`, `load_notes`, `export_notes_zstd`

Concept Overview

A module is a single `.py` file. A package is a directory containing an `__init__.py` file (and usually more modules). Together they form the unit of organization in Python. Up to this point, the Personal Knowledge Tracker CLI has lived in chapter-specific files such as `ch06_io.py`. That works for learning, but it does not scale. Real applications separate concerns so that storage logic does not leak into CLI parsing and domain models do not depend on the file system.

This chapter refactors the tracker into a proper `src/knowledge_tracker/` package with four internal modules. `models` holds data definitions and validation without side effects, while `storage` handles paths, JSON, and Zstandard compression. `commands` implements the operations users invoke, and `cli` parses arguments and dispatches to commands. The dependency graph is strictly one way: `cli` imports `commands`; `commands` imports `models` and `storage`; `storage` imports `models`; `models` imports nothing from the application. Violating this rule invites circular imports.

Source layout places the package under a `src/` directory. This prevents Python from importing the raw package directory during development, which ensures that tests and imports exercise the installed package rather than the local source. Modern tooling, including `uv` and `pytest`, expects this structure.

Flat layout once cost me three sprints of CI failures that local imports masked completely during development. Source layout catches these packaging errors early.

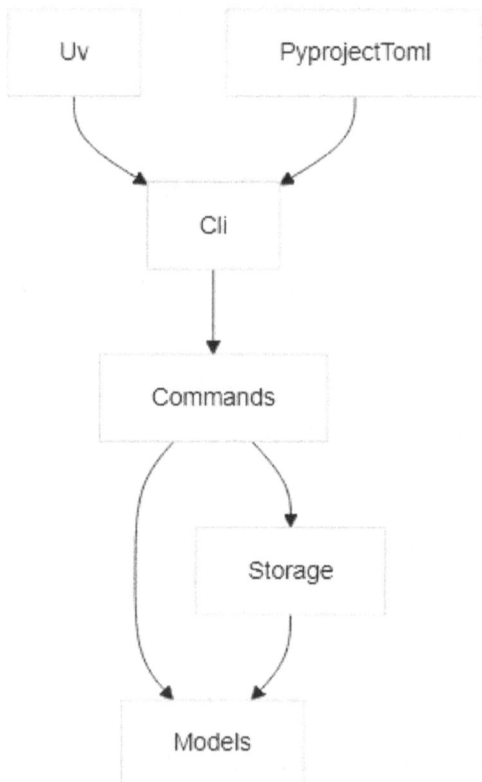

The arrows in the diagram point downward: `cli` calls into `commands`, `commands` calls into `storage` and `models`, and `storage` calls into `models`. No arrow points upward. A reverse edge, such as `storage` importing `cli` to log a message, or `models` importing `storage` to load defaults, breaks the acyclic graph and triggers an `ImportError` at runtime. Keep every import arrow pointing downward.

Step-by-Step Implementation

Step 1: Configure Source Layout and Package Discovery

When `uv init` created the project in Chapter 1, it generated a `src/knowledge_tracker/` directory and a `pyproject.toml` with a `[project]` table. Ensure you initialized the project with `uv init` in its default package mode, which produces the `src/` directory and project metadata automatically.

To make the directory a discoverable package, the build system must know where to look. Python packaging uses a build backend (here, `hatchling`) to transform source files into an installable distribution. The backend reads `pyproject.toml` to find the `[build-system]` table, which declares the backend dependency and entry point. The `[tool.hatch.build.targets.wheel]` table tells `hatchling` which directories to include in the wheel. The `packages` key points to `src/knowledge_tracker`. After installation, `import knowledge_tracker` resolves correctly. Without this metadata, the installed package would omit the module entirely, so `import knowledge_tracker` will fail.

Packaging metadata is not optional.

Inspect your `pyproject.toml` and ensure it contains these sections:

```
[project]
name = "knowledge-tracker"
version = "0.1.0"
description = "Personal Knowledge Tracker CLI"
requires-python = ">=3.14"

[build-system]
requires = ["hatchling"]
build-backend = "hatchling.build"

[tool.hatch.build.targets.wheel]
packages = ["src/knowledge_tracker"]
```

After verifying or adding the missing sections, run `uv sync` to install the project into the virtual environment in editable mode. Changes in `src/knowledge_tracker/` are then reflected immediately without reinstallation.

Your directory tree should look like this:

```
knowledge-tracker/
├── pyproject.toml
├── .python-version
├── uv.lock
├── src/
│   └── knowledge_tracker/
│       ├── __init__.py
│       ├── __main__.py
│       ├── models.py
│       ├── storage.py
│       ├── commands.py
│       └── cli.py
└── tests/
    └── ...
```

The `tests/` directory stays empty for now; the test suite lands in Chapter 11.

Never use flat layout for new projects. It places the package directory at the repository root, causing Python to import the local folder before the installed package and hiding packaging errors until deployment. Source layout under `src/<package>/` avoids this entirely.

Step 2: Declare Third-Party Dependencies

Adding a dependency is a declaration, not a manual edit. Use `uv add` and let the tool record the requirement, resolve a compatible version, update `pyproject.toml`, and refresh `uv.lock` in one step. Editing `pyproject.toml` by hand and hoping the lockfile catches up is how environments drift.

The tracker fetches metadata for notes that carry a `source_url`, so add an HTTP client as a runtime dependency:

```
uv add httpx
```

Test-only tools should not ship with the application. Declare them in a dependency group instead, so they install during development but stay out of the published wheel:

```
uv add --dev pytest
```

After both commands, your `pyproject.toml` carries a PEP 621 `dependencies` list under `[project]` and a `dev` list under `[dependency-groups]`:

```
[project]
name = "knowledge-tracker"
version = "0.1.0"
description = "Personal Knowledge Tracker CLI"
requires-python = ">=3.14"
dependencies = [
    "httpx>=0.28",
]

[dependency-groups]
dev = [
    "pytest>=8.3",
]
```

Runtime dependencies belong in `[project] dependencies` and ship with the wheel. Development dependencies belong in `[dependency-groups] dev` and never reach end users. The test suite in Chapter 11 relies on this `dev` group.

Declare dependencies, do not hand-edit lockfiles.

Step 3: Extract Domain Models

The domain layer belongs in `src/knowledge_tracker/models.py`. This module owns the `NoteDict` alias and every function that operates on note data without performing file I/O, CLI parsing, or mutating process-level state. Keeping models free of these concerns means any other layer can import them safely.

The `NoteDict` contract from Chapter 2 remains unchanged: it describes dictionaries with string keys and values that may be strings, string lists, or `None`. The following functions move here from earlier chapters.

```
from datetime import datetime, timezone

type NoteDict = dict[str, str | list[str] | None]

def create_note(
    title: str,
    body: str,
    tags: list[str],
    source_url: str | None = None,
) -> NoteDict:
    return {
        "title": title,
        "body": body,
        "tags": tags,
        "created": datetime.now(tz=timezone.utc).isoformat(),
        "source_url": source_url,
```

```
    }

def is_valid_note(note: NoteDict) -> bool:
    title = note.get("title")
    body = note.get("body")
    return (
        isinstance(title, str)
        and isinstance(body, str)
        and bool(title.strip())
        and bool(body.strip())
    )

def format_tags(tags: list[str]) -> str:
    if not tags:
        return "no tags"
    return ", ".join(f"#{t}" for t in tags)

def preview_note(note: NoteDict) -> str:
    title = note.get("title", "")
    tags = note.get("tags")
    if not isinstance(tags, list):
        tags = []
    tag_str = format_tags([t for t in tags if isinstance(t, str)])
    return f"{title} [{tag_str}]"

def summarize_notes(notes: list[NoteDict], limit: int | None = None)
-> str:
    previews: list[str] = []
    for note in notes:
        if not is_valid_note(note):
            continue
        previews.append(preview_note(note))
        if limit is not None and len(previews) == limit:
            break
    return "\n".join(previews) if previews else "No notes found"

def filter_by_tag(notes: list[NoteDict], tag: str) -> list[NoteDict]:
    return [
        n
        for n in notes
        if isinstance(n.get("tags"), list)
        and any(isinstance(t, str) and t.lower() == tag.lower() for t
in n["tags"])
    ]
```

No module in `models` should ever import `storage` or `cli`. All names here are functions and a type alias that depend only on the standard library. Relocating these definitions into a single module makes the data contract explicit and greppable.

Greppable contracts save time.

Step 4: Isolate Persistence

Persistence code moves to `src/knowledge_tracker/storage.py`. This layer imports `NoteDict` from `models` and handles every interaction with the file system.

```
import json
from compression.zstd import compress
from pathlib import Path

from knowledge_tracker.models import NoteDict
```

`compression.zstd` is part of the Python 3.14 standard library, so it sits in the same import group as `json` and `pathlib`. The blank line separates the standard-library imports from the local application import. The one-shot `compress` function returns the complete compressed frame in a single call, so there is no compressor object to flush.

```
def get_data_dir() -> Path:
    return Path.home() / ".knowledge_tracker"

def get_notes_file(data_dir: Path | None = None) -> Path:
    target = data_dir or get_data_dir()
    target.mkdir(parents=True, exist_ok=True)
    return target / "notes.json"

def save_notes(notes: list[NoteDict], path: Path | None = None) ->
None:
    target = path or get_notes_file()
    with open(target, "w", encoding="utf-8") as f:
        json.dump(notes, f, indent=2, ensure_ascii=False)

def load_notes(path: Path | None = None) -> list[NoteDict]:
    target = path or get_notes_file()
    try:
        with open(target, "r", encoding="utf-8") as f:
            data = json.load(f)
    except (FileNotFoundError, json.JSONDecodeError):
        return []
    if not isinstance(data, list):
        return []
    return [item for item in data if isinstance(item, dict)]

def export_notes_zstd(notes: list[NoteDict], archive_path: Path) ->
None:
    archive_path.parent.mkdir(parents=True, exist_ok=True)
    payload = json.dumps(notes, indent=2,
ensure_ascii=False).encode("utf-8")
    compressed = compress(payload)
```

```
    with open(archive_path, "wb") as f:
        f.write(compressed)
```

By confining `Path` operations, JSON serialization, and Zstandard compression to this module, the rest of the application remains unaware of how notes are stored. Swapping JSON for SQLite later would require changes only in `storage.py`.

Storage details belong here alone.

Step 5: Wire Command Handlers

Command handlers live in `src/knowledge_tracker/commands.py`. This module bridges domain logic and persistence, importing from `models` and `storage` but never from `cli`. It may depend on `argparse` because it sits at the boundary between CLI structures and domain logic. `models` and `storage` never import `argparse`.

```
import argparse
from pathlib import Path

from knowledge_tracker.models import (
    NoteDict,
    create_note,
    filter_by_tag,
    is_valid_note,
    preview_note,
    summarize_notes,
)
from knowledge_tracker.storage import (
    export_notes_zstd,
    get_notes_file,
    load_notes,
    save_notes,
)

def run_search(notes: list[NoteDict], args: argparse.Namespace) ->
str:
    results = list(notes)
    tag = getattr(args, "tag", None)
    if tag:
        results = filter_by_tag(results, tag)
    query = args.query.lower()
    matches = [
        n
        for n in results
        if isinstance(n, dict)
```

```
        and (
            query in str(n.get("title", "")).lower()
            or query in str(n.get("body", "")).lower()
            or query in str(n.get("source_url", "")).lower()
        )
    ]
    return summarize_notes(matches)
```

`run_search` defensively copies the input list, then filters by tag and query text. It coerces title, body, and source URL values to strings before calling `.lower()`, so malformed note data cannot raise an `AttributeError`.

```
def run_create_persisted(args: argparse.Namespace) -> str:
    notes = load_notes()
    title = args.title.strip()
    body = args.body.strip()
    if not title or not body:
        return "Error: title and body cannot be empty."
    note = create_note(title, body, args.tag or [], getattr(args,
"source_url", None))
    if not is_valid_note(note):
        return "Error: note validation failed."
    notes.append(note)
    try:
        save_notes(notes)
    except OSError as e:
        return f"Error: failed to save note ({e})."
    return f"Created note: {preview_note(note)}"

def run_list_persisted(args: argparse.Namespace) -> str:
    notes = load_notes()
    limit = getattr(args, "limit", None)
    if limit is not None:
        if limit <= 0:
            return "Error: limit must be positive."
        return summarize_notes(notes, limit=limit)
    return summarize_notes(notes)

def run_search_persisted(args: argparse.Namespace) -> str:
    notes = load_notes()
    return run_search(notes, args)

def run_export_persisted(args: argparse.Namespace) -> str:
    notes = load_notes()
    output = getattr(args, "output", None)
    if output:
        archive_path = Path(output)
    else:
        archive_path = get_notes_file().with_suffix(".json.zst")
    try:
        export_notes_zstd(notes, archive_path)
```

```
    except OSError as e:
        return f"Error: failed to export notes ({e})."
    return f"Exported {len(notes)} notes to {archive_path}"
```

Each handler loads data, performs domain operations, persists changes, and returns a status string. Keeping `argparse` usage inside `commands.py` is acceptable because this module already orchestrates user-facing operations; pushing `Namespace` objects into `models` would violate layer boundaries.

Keep CLI structures out of models.

Step 6: Build the CLI Entry Point

The CLI entry point is `src/knowledge_tracker/cli.py`. This is the only application module that knows about `argparse` and console output. It imports from `commands` and dispatches.

```
import argparse

from knowledge_tracker.commands import (
    run_create_persisted,
    run_export_persisted,
    run_list_persisted,
    run_search_persisted,
)

def build_persisted_parser() -> argparse.ArgumentParser:
    parser = argparse.ArgumentParser(prog="knowledge-tracker")
    subparsers = parser.add_subparsers(dest="command", required=True)

    create = subparsers.add_parser("create")
    create.add_argument("title")
    create.add_argument("body")
    create.add_argument("--tag", action="append", default=[])
    create.add_argument("--source-url", default=None)

    list_ = subparsers.add_parser("list")
    list_.add_argument("--limit", type=int, default=None)

    search = subparsers.add_parser("search")
    search.add_argument("query")
    search.add_argument("--tag", default=None)

    export = subparsers.add_parser("export")
    export.add_argument("--output", default=None)

    return parser
```

```
def run_persisted_cli() -> None:
    parser = build_persisted_parser()
    args = parser.parse_args()
    match args.command:
        case "create":
            print(run_create_persisted(args))
        case "list":
            print(run_list_persisted(args))
        case "search":
            print(run_search_persisted(args))
        case "export":
            print(run_export_persisted(args))
        case _:
            print("Unknown command")
```

Because `cli` sits at the top of the dependency graph, nothing inside `models`, `storage`, or `commands` imports it. If `storage` ever imported `cli` to print a message, and `cli` imported `storage` to load data, Python would raise an `ImportError` at runtime.

Cycles always surface as `ImportError`.

Individual modules remain importable. If you run a single file directly during debugging, any module-level side effects would execute immediately. Keep module bodies free of top-level calls, and retain `if __name__ == "__main__"` guards in any script that doubles as a module to prevent accidental execution on import.

Step 7: Expose the Package Interface

Finally, expose the package with `src/knowledge_tracker/__init__.py` and `__main__.py`. The `__init__.py` file makes the directory a package. It also defines `__all__`, which tells readers and linters exactly what the package considers public.

```
__all__ = [
    "models",
    "storage",
    "commands",
    "cli",
]
```

Create `src/knowledge_tracker/__main__.py` so the package can be executed directly:

```
from knowledge_tracker.cli import run_persisted_cli

if __name__ == "__main__":
    run_persisted_cli()
```

With this file in place, `uv run python -m knowledge_tracker` resolves the package, runs `__main__.py`, and invokes the CLI. No shell script or manual `sys.path` manipulation is required. The `if __name__ == "__main__"` guard ensures that importing the package does not trigger CLI execution.

Importing the package stays safe.

Full Example

The following listings consolidate the entire refactored package. Copy these files into the tree from Step 1 and run `uv run python -m knowledge_tracker --help`.

`src/knowledge_tracker/__init__.py`:

```
__all__ = [
    "models",
    "storage",
    "commands",
    "cli",
]
```

`src/knowledge_tracker/__main__.py`:

```
from knowledge_tracker.cli import run_persisted_cli

if __name__ == "__main__":
    run_persisted_cli()
```

`src/knowledge_tracker/models.py`:

```
from datetime import datetime, timezone

type NoteDict = dict[str, str | list[str] | None]

def create_note(
    title: str,
    body: str,
    tags: list[str],
```

```
    source_url: str | None = None,
) -> NoteDict:
    return {
        "title": title,
        "body": body,
        "tags": tags,
        "created": datetime.now(tz=timezone.utc).isoformat(),
        "source_url": source_url,
    }

def is_valid_note(note: NoteDict) -> bool:
    title = note.get("title")
    body = note.get("body")
    return (
        isinstance(title, str)
        and isinstance(body, str)
        and bool(title.strip())
        and bool(body.strip())
    )

def format_tags(tags: list[str]) -> str:
    if not tags:
        return "no tags"
    return ", ".join(f"#{t}" for t in tags)

def preview_note(note: NoteDict) -> str:
    title = note.get("title", "")
    tags = note.get("tags")
    if not isinstance(tags, list):
        tags = []
    tag_str = format_tags([t for t in tags if isinstance(t, str)])
    return f"{title} [{tag_str}]"

def summarize_notes(notes: list[NoteDict], limit: int | None = None)
-> str:
    previews: list[str] = []
    for note in notes:
        if not is_valid_note(note):
            continue
        previews.append(preview_note(note))
        if limit is not None and len(previews) == limit:
            break
    return "\n".join(previews) if previews else "No notes found"

def filter_by_tag(notes: list[NoteDict], tag: str) -> list[NoteDict]:
    return [
        n
        for n in notes
        if isinstance(n.get("tags"), list)
        and any(isinstance(t, str) and t.lower() == tag.lower() for t
in n["tags"])
    ]
```

src/knowledge_tracker/storage.py:

```
import json
from compression.zstd import compress
from pathlib import Path

from knowledge_tracker.models import NoteDict

def get_data_dir() -> Path:
    return Path.home() / ".knowledge_tracker"

def get_notes_file(data_dir: Path | None = None) -> Path:
    target = data_dir or get_data_dir()
    target.mkdir(parents=True, exist_ok=True)
    return target / "notes.json"

def save_notes(notes: list[NoteDict], path: Path | None = None) ->
None:
    target = path or get_notes_file()
    with open(target, "w", encoding="utf-8") as f:
        json.dump(notes, f, indent=2, ensure_ascii=False)

def load_notes(path: Path | None = None) -> list[NoteDict]:
    target = path or get_notes_file()
    try:
        with open(target, "r", encoding="utf-8") as f:
            data = json.load(f)
    except (FileNotFoundError, json.JSONDecodeError):
        return []
    if not isinstance(data, list):
        return []
    return [item for item in data if isinstance(item, dict)]

def export_notes_zstd(notes: list[NoteDict], archive_path: Path) ->
None:
    archive_path.parent.mkdir(parents=True, exist_ok=True)
    payload = json.dumps(notes, indent=2,
ensure_ascii=False).encode("utf-8")
    compressed = compress(payload)
    with open(archive_path, "wb") as f:
        f.write(compressed)
```

src/knowledge_tracker/commands.py:

```
import argparse
from pathlib import Path

from knowledge_tracker.models import (
    NoteDict,
    create_note,
    filter_by_tag,
    is_valid_note,
```

```
    preview_note,
    summarize_notes,
)
from knowledge_tracker.storage import (
    export_notes_zstd,
    get_notes_file,
    load_notes,
    save_notes,
)

def run_search(notes: list[NoteDict], args: argparse.Namespace) ->
str:
    results = list(notes)
    tag = getattr(args, "tag", None)
    if tag:
        results = filter_by_tag(results, tag)
    query = args.query.lower()
    matches = [
        n
        for n in results
        if isinstance(n, dict)
        and (
            query in str(n.get("title", "")).lower()
            or query in str(n.get("body", "")).lower()
            or query in str(n.get("source_url", "")).lower()
        )
    ]
    return summarize_notes(matches)

def run_create_persisted(args: argparse.Namespace) -> str:
    notes = load_notes()
    title = args.title.strip()
    body = args.body.strip()
    if not title or not body:
        return "Error: title and body cannot be empty."
    note = create_note(title, body, args.tag or [], getattr(args,
"source_url", None))
    if not is_valid_note(note):
        return "Error: note validation failed."
    notes.append(note)
    try:
        save_notes(notes)
    except OSError as e:
        return f"Error: failed to save note ({e})."
    return f"Created note: {preview_note(note)}"

def run_list_persisted(args: argparse.Namespace) -> str:
    notes = load_notes()
    limit = getattr(args, "limit", None)
    if limit is not None:
        if limit <= 0:
            return "Error: limit must be positive."
        return summarize_notes(notes, limit=limit)
    return summarize_notes(notes)
```

```
def run_search_persisted(args: argparse.Namespace) -> str:
    notes = load_notes()
    return run_search(notes, args)

def run_export_persisted(args: argparse.Namespace) -> str:
    notes = load_notes()
    output = getattr(args, "output", None)
    if output:
        archive_path = Path(output)
    else:
        archive_path = get_notes_file().with_suffix(".json.zst")
    try:
        export_notes_zstd(notes, archive_path)
    except OSError as e:
        return f"Error: failed to export notes ({e})."
    return f"Exported {len(notes)} notes to {archive_path}"
```

src/knowledge_tracker/cli.py:

```
import argparse

from knowledge_tracker.commands import (
    run_create_persisted,
    run_export_persisted,
    run_list_persisted,
    run_search_persisted,
)

def build_persisted_parser() -> argparse.ArgumentParser:
    parser = argparse.ArgumentParser(prog="knowledge-tracker")
    subparsers = parser.add_subparsers(dest="command", required=True)

    create = subparsers.add_parser("create")
    create.add_argument("title")
    create.add_argument("body")
    create.add_argument("--tag", action="append", default=[])
    create.add_argument("--source-url", default=None)

    list_ = subparsers.add_parser("list")
    list_.add_argument("--limit", type=int, default=None)

    search = subparsers.add_parser("search")
    search.add_argument("query")
    search.add_argument("--tag", default=None)

    export = subparsers.add_parser("export")
    export.add_argument("--output", default=None)

    return parser

def run_persisted_cli() -> None:
```

```
    parser = build_persisted_parser()
    args = parser.parse_args()
    match args.command:
        case "create":
            print(run_create_persisted(args))
        case "list":
            print(run_list_persisted(args))
        case "search":
            print(run_search_persisted(args))
        case "export":
            print(run_export_persisted(args))
        case _:
            print("Unknown command")
```

This layout enforces a strict boundary: `models` knows nothing of the file system, `storage` knows nothing of argument parsing, and `cli` knows nothing of JSON or Zstandard. Each layer communicates through well-defined function signatures and the `NoteDict` type. When Chapter 8 replaces `NoteDict` with a dataclass, only `models` and the type signatures in `storage` and `commands` will change. The architecture remains intact.

Common Mistakes

- **Never use flat layout for new projects.** It places the package directory at the repository root, causing Python to import the local folder before the installed package and hiding packaging errors until deployment. Use `src/<package>/` for every new project.
- **Circular imports kill startup.** They occur when two modules depend on each other directly or transitively. If `storage` imports `cli` to print a message while `cli` imports `storage` to load data, Python cannot resolve either module. Keep the dependency graph acyclic; `models` must remain the leaf layer.
- **Always include `__init__.py` in regular application packages.** Python 3.3 introduced implicit namespace packages, which allow directories without `__init__.py` to act as packages. This is useful for splitting a single logical package across multiple directories, but it complicates discovery and can confuse static type checkers.
- **Absolute imports are unambiguous.** They specify the full dotted path from the project root and work with `python -m`, `pytest`, and `mypy`

without path gymnastics. Relative imports break when a module is executed directly as a script, so avoid them in application code.

- **Treat `__all__` as a public API contract and keep it current.** When `__all__` is present, `from knowledge_tracker import *` exports only the names listed. If you add a new public submodule and omit it from `__all__`, consumers cannot discover it through wildcard imports.

Performance and Production Considerations

Package structure has minimal runtime overhead, but it has significant maintenance impact.

Import order affects startup time. Python executes module-level code on first import. Heavy computation at the top of `models` or `storage` slows every CLI invocation. Keep module bodies lightweight; defer work into functions.

Keep the feedback loop tight with editable installs. `uv sync` installs the project in editable mode by default, so changes to `src/knowledge_tracker/` are active immediately without reinstalling. Do not manipulate `sys.path` in application code to point at source directories; that bypasses the packaging metadata and breaks in containers.

You can search and refactor faster with absolute imports. A codebase that uses `from knowledge_tracker.storage import load_notes` is easier to grep than one that uses `from .storage import load_notes`. I lost an hour last month fixing relative imports after a module broke under `pytest` in CI. Prefer absolute imports in application code.

Tests stay fast when boundaries are clean. When `commands` depends only on `models` and `storage`, you can test command logic with an in-memory list and a temporary path. If `commands` reaches into `cli` or global state, tests require full parser construction and become slow.

Summary

This chapter transformed the Personal Knowledge Tracker CLI from a collection of chapter scripts into a maintainable `src/knowledge_tracker/` package. Source layout prevents accidental top-level imports. The installed package is what runs.

Four internal modules, `models`, `storage`, `commands`, and `cli`, separate domain logic from persistence and user interface concerns. Absolute imports wire the layers together without circular dependencies. `__init__.py` marks directories as packages, `__all__` defines the public contract, and `__main__.py` enables execution via `uv run python -m knowledge_tracker`. The structure is now ready for the dataclass refactor in Chapter 8 and the test suite in Chapter 11.

Key Terms

- **Module**: a single `.py` file containing Python definitions and statements.
- **Package**: a directory of Python modules that includes an `__init__.py` file, forming a namespace for imports.
- **Source layout**: a project structure that places packages under a `src/` directory; this ensures tests exercise the installed package rather than raw source files.
- **Absolute import**: an import statement that specifies the full dotted path from the project root (e.g., `from knowledge_tracker.models import NoteDict`); preferred over relative imports in application code.
- **Circular import**: a runtime error that occurs when two or more modules import each other directly or transitively, preventing Python from resolving either module fully.
- **`__init__.py`**: a file that marks a directory as a Python package and executes package-level initialization on first import.
- **`__all__`**: a list of names that defines the public interface exposed by `from module import *`.
- **`__main__.py`**: a file inside a package that enables execution via `python -m package_name` by serving as the entry point.
- **Editable install**: a package installation mode, used by default with `uv sync`, where changes to source files are reflected immediately without reinstallation.

Mini Quiz

1. **What is the primary benefit of using source layout (`src/<package>/`) for the Personal Knowledge Tracker CLI?**

   A. It eliminates the need for a `pyproject.toml` file.

   B. It ensures that imports and tests exercise the installed package instead of the raw source directory.

   C. It allows the package to run on Python versions older than 3.14.

   D. It removes the requirement for `__init__.py` files inside package directories.

2. **In `src/knowledge_tracker/commands.py`, the line `from knowledge_tracker.models import NoteDict` is an example of which import style?**

   A. A relative import because it references a sibling module.

   B. An absolute import that requires the package to be installed or on `PYTHONPATH`.

   C. An implicit namespace import that works without `__init__.py`.

   D. A conditional import that defers resolution until runtime.

3. **A developer creates a new `analytics.py` module inside `src/knowledge_tracker/` and writes `from knowledge_tracker.cli import run_persisted_cli` at the top level. The `cli.py` module already imports `from knowledge_tracker.commands import ...`, and `commands.py` imports `from knowledge_tracker.analytics import ...`. What will happen when the application starts?**

   A. Python will ignore the duplicate imports and start normally.

   B. An `ImportError` or `AttributeError` will occur because of a circular import.

   C. The application will start, but `uv sync` will fail to create the lockfile.

   D. The modules will load in alphabetical order, so `analytics.py` will always resolve first.

4. **Which file inside `src/knowledge_tracker/` makes it possible to run the application with `uv run python -m knowledge_tracker`?**

   A. `__init__.py`

   B. `__all__.py`

C. `__main__.py`

D. `pyproject.toml`

5. **What is the purpose of the `__all__` list defined in `src/knowledge_tracker/__init__.py`?**

   A. It registers CLI subcommands for the argument parser.

   B. It restricts which names are exported when `from knowledge_tracker import *` is used.

   C. It tells the build backend which modules to compile into the wheel.

   D. It prevents circular imports by blocking cross-module references.

Answers are provided in the Answer Key at the end of the book.

Activity

Extend the Personal Knowledge Tracker CLI with a new `stats` subcommand that reports the total number of valid notes and the count of unique tags. This exercise reinforces creating a new package module, using absolute imports, and maintaining the one-way dependency graph. You'll place `stats.py` at the leaf of the dependency graph; it may import from `models` but must not import from `cli`, `commands`, or `storage`.

- Create a new file at `src/knowledge_tracker/stats.py`. Define a pure function `compute_stats(notes: list[NoteDict]) -> dict[str, int]` that returns `{"total": total_valid_notes, "unique_tags": unique_tag_count}`. Import `NoteDict` and `is_valid_note` from `knowledge_tracker.models`. Compute the unique tag count by iterating over valid notes, normalizing each tag with `.strip().lower()`, and skipping non-string entries.
- Open `src/knowledge_tracker/commands.py`. Add a new function `run_stats_persisted(args: argparse.Namespace) -> str` that calls `load_notes()`, passes the result to `compute_stats`, and returns a formatted string such as `"Total notes: 5 | Unique tags: 3"`. Import `compute_stats` from `knowledge_tracker.stats` at the top of the module.
- Open `src/knowledge_tracker/cli.py`. Register a new `"stats"` subparser in `build_persisted_parser()` that takes no additional arguments. Extend the `match` block in `run_persisted_cli()` to dispatch the `"stats"` command to `run_stats_persisted`.
- Run `uv sync` to refresh the editable install, then create a test note with `uv run python -m knowledge_tracker create "Activity Test" "Testing stats" --tag python --tag uv`. Execute `uv run python -m knowledge_tracker stats` and verify the output shows one total note and two unique tags.
- Confirm that `stats.py` remains a leaf module by ensuring it does not import from `cli`, `commands`, or `storage`. This preserves the acyclic dependency graph established in this chapter.

Chapter 8: Classes, Dataclasses, and Protocols

What You Will Learn

- Replace dictionary-based note data with type-safe `@dataclass` models
- Attach domain behavior to data with methods and `@property`
- Use dataclass inheritance and `@override` to extend base entities
- Define a `Protocol` to express storage boundaries without forcing inheritance
- Implement an in-memory repository for fast testing and a JSON-backed repository for persistence
- Refactor command handlers to depend on a repository interface rather than concrete storage

Prerequisites

- Completion of Chapter 7 (source-layout packages, absolute imports, and the four-layer module graph)
- Completion of Chapter 6 (`pathlib`, JSON serialization, Zstandard compression, and defensive loading)
- Completion of Chapter 4 (typed function signatures, keyword-only arguments, and deferred annotation evaluation)
- Completion of Chapter 3 (`argparse` subparsers and command routing)

Concept Overview

The Personal Knowledge Tracker CLI currently passes note data as dictionaries. Dictionaries are flexible, but they defer error detection to runtime; a typo in a key or a wrong type flows silently until something crashes. Classes bundle data with behavior and give you field names that static analyzers can verify.

I once traced a production bug to a `note['titel']` typo that survived code review because dictionary access is always valid syntax.

Python 3.14 retains the standard `@dataclass` decorator from earlier releases. It generates `__init__`, `__repr__`, and `__eq__` from field declarations, removing boilerplate while keeping the type checker in the loop. You add methods and properties directly to the class, so validation and formatting live next to the fields they operate on.

Inheritance lets you share structure across entities. A `BaseEntity` can own `id` and `created`; a `Note` subclass adds `title`, `body`, and `tags`. Mark overridden methods with `@override` from the `typing` module. That single decorator makes intent explicit. Type checkers report mismatches immediately when a parent signature changes.

Protocols complete the picture. A `Protocol` defines an interface by shape, not by inheritance. Any class that implements the required methods is a valid substitute at type-check time. This is structural subtyping; it is the Pythonic way to invert dependencies. Command handlers should ask for a `NoteRepository`, not a `JsonNoteRepository`.

Avoid dicts for domain models. The lack of field safety creates maintenance debt.

Step-by-Step Implementation

Step 1: Domain Type Aliases and Base Dataclass

Start with narrow type aliases and a small base class that every entity will share.

```
from dataclasses import dataclass

type NoteId = str
type Tag = str

@dataclass
class BaseEntity:
    id: NoteId
    created: str

    def to_dict(self) -> dict[str, object]:
        return {"id": self.id, "created": self.created}
```

`NoteId` and `Tag` are semantic wrappers around `str`. They do not change runtime behavior, but they clarify intent for readers and type checkers. `BaseEntity` declares the two fields every persisted record needs, plus a serialization helper.

Step 2: Note Dataclass with Inheritance and Behavior

Subclass `BaseEntity` to form the `Note` model. Add a property for source validation, a `preview` method, and override `to_dict`. A property is accessed like an attribute; `note.has_source` yields a boolean without parentheses.

```
from typing import override

@dataclass
class Note(BaseEntity):
    title: str
    body: str
    tags: list[Tag]
    source_url: str | None = None

    @property
    def has_source(self) -> bool:
        return self.source_url is not None and
self.source_url.startswith(("http://", "https://"))

    @override
    def to_dict(self) -> dict[str, object]:
        base = super().to_dict()
        base.update({
            "title": self.title,
            "body": self.body,
            "tags": self.tags,
            "source_url": self.source_url,
        })
        return base

    def preview(self) -> str:
        tag_line = ", ".join(f"#{t}" for t in self.tags) if self.tags
else "no tags"
        return f"{self.title} [{tag_line}]"
```

Dataclass inheritance enforces a strict rule. Fields without defaults must appear before fields with defaults, and inherited fields always come first. `BaseEntity` defines no defaults, so `Note` can safely add `source_url: str |`

`None = None` after its required fields. Had `BaseEntity` carried a default, a new required field in `Note` would trigger a `TypeError` immediately.

Step 3: SearchQuery and Dataclass Helpers

Introduce a `SearchQuery` dataclass to replace ad hoc query strings and tag lists. Then add new construction, validation, and preview helpers that operate on `Note` instances. The existing `create_note`, `is_valid_note`, and `preview_note` functions from earlier chapters continue to work with `NoteDict` dictionaries; these new helpers are for the dataclass layer.

```
from datetime import datetime, timezone

def _utc_now() -> str:
    return datetime.now(timezone.utc).isoformat()

def _make_note_id(title: str) -> NoteId:
    safe = "".join(c if c.isalnum() else "_" for c in title.lower())
    ts = datetime.now(timezone.utc).strftime("%Y%m%d%H%M%S%f")
    return f"note-{safe}-{ts}"

@dataclass
class SearchQuery:
    text: str = ""
    tags: list[Tag] | None = None
    limit: int | None = None

def make_note(
    title: str,
    body: str,
    tags: list[Tag],
    source_url: str | None = None,
) -> Note:
    return Note(
        id=_make_note_id(title),
        created=_utc_now(),
        title=title,
        body=body,
        tags=[t.strip().lower() for t in tags if t.strip()],
        source_url=source_url,
    )

def note_is_valid(note: Note) -> bool:
    return bool(note.title.strip()) and bool(note.body.strip())

def format_note_preview(note: Note) -> str:
    return note.preview()
```

make_note returns a Note instead of a NoteDict. note_is_valid accesses attributes, not dictionary keys. format_note_preview delegates to the instance method, keeping the rendering rule inside the model where it belongs.

Step 4: Repository Protocol

Define the storage boundary as a protocol. Any class that implements save, list_all, and search satisfies this interface, regardless of its inheritance chain. The ... (Ellipsis) in each method body declares that the method is part of the interface without providing an implementation.

```
from pathlib import Path
from typing import Protocol

class NoteRepository(Protocol):
    path: Path | None

    def save(self, note: Note) -> None:
        ...

    def list_all(self) -> list[Note]:
        ...

    def search(self, query: SearchQuery) -> list[Note]:
        ...
```

Protocols are checked statically by tools like mypy. At runtime, CPython ignores them unless you opt into runtime_checkable. Keep them lean; they should describe operations, not implementation details.

Step 5: In-Memory Implementation

Build a concrete repository that stores notes in a private list. This implementation is ideal for unit tests because it avoids disk I/O entirely.

```
class InMemoryNoteRepository:
    def __init__(self) -> None:
        self._notes: list[Note] = []
        self.path: Path | None = None

    def save(self, note: Note) -> None:
        self._notes.append(note)

    def list_all(self) -> list[Note]:
        return list(self._notes)
```

```
    def search(self, query: SearchQuery) -> list[Note]:
        results = self._notes
        if query.tags:
            results = [
                n for n in results
                if all(t.lower() in (tag.lower() for tag in n.tags)
for t in query.tags)
            ]
        if query.text:
            q = query.text.lower()
            results = [
                n for n in results
                if q in n.title.lower()
                or q in n.body.lower()
                or (n.source_url and q in n.source_url.lower())
            ]
        if query.limit is not None and query.limit > 0:
            results = results[:query.limit]
        return list(results)
```

The leading underscore on `_notes` signals that the attribute is private. Consumers should interact with the repository through its public methods, not by reaching into the list. Tag matching is case-insensitive so that queries align with normalized tags.

Step 6: File-Backed Repository with Inheritance

Subclass `InMemoryNoteRepository` to add JSON persistence. Load existing data during initialization, and override `save` to flush changes to disk.

The `_load` method reads the JSON file, validates that the top-level value is a list, and reconstructs `Note` instances only from dictionary items. Each field is coerced to its expected type so malformed entries fail gracefully inside the `try` block. Tags are validated as a list, stripped, lowercased, and blank strings are discarded.

Defensive loading prevents one corrupt record from destroying the entire store.

```
import json

class JsonNoteRepository(InMemoryNoteRepository):
    def __init__(self, path: Path | None = None) -> None:
        super().__init__()
        self._path = path or Path.home() / ".knowledge_tracker" /
"notes.json"
        self.path = self._path
```

```
        self._load()

    def _load(self) -> None:
        if not self._path.exists():
            return
        try:
            with self._path.open("r", encoding="utf-8") as f:
                data = json.load(f)
        except (json.JSONDecodeError, OSError):
            return
        if not isinstance(data, list):
            return
        for item in data:
            if not isinstance(item, dict):
                continue
            try:
                raw_tags = item.get("tags", [])
                tags: list[str] = []
                if isinstance(raw_tags, list):
                    tags = [
                        str(t).strip().lower()
                        for t in raw_tags
                        if isinstance(t, str) and str(t).strip()
                    ]
                note = Note(
                    id=str(item.get("id", "")),
                    created=str(item.get("created", "")),
                    title=str(item.get("title", "")),
                    body=str(item.get("body", "")),
                    tags=tags,
                    source_url=item.get("source_url") if
isinstance(item.get("source_url"), str) else None,
                )
                self._notes.append(note)
            except (TypeError, ValueError):
                continue

    @override
    def save(self, note: Note) -> None:
        super().save(note)
        self._persist()

    def _persist(self) -> None:
        self._path.parent.mkdir(parents=True, exist_ok=True)
        with self._path.open("w", encoding="utf-8") as f:
            json.dump([n.to_dict() for n in self._notes], f,
indent=2, ensure_ascii=False)
```

`JsonNoteRepository` reuses the search and list logic from its parent. It only overrides the points where persistence matters: initialization and `save`. The `@override` decorator tells mypy to verify that `save` actually exists on

`InMemoryNoteRepository`. If a refactor renames the parent method, the type checker catches the stale subclass.

Step 7: Command Handlers Refactored Behind the Protocol

Rewrite the command handlers to accept a `NoteRepository` instead of a raw note list. The handlers below expect an `argparse.Namespace` with these attributes: `title` and `body` strings for create; `tag` as a list of strings; optional `source_url` for create; optional `limit` for list and search; `query` string for search; and optional `output` path for export.

Always inject repositories. Hard-coding storage inside handlers makes testing impossible.

```
import argparse

def run_create_repo(repo: NoteRepository, args: argparse.Namespace) -
> str:
    title = args.title.strip()
    body = args.body.strip()
    if not title or not body:
        return "Error: title and body cannot be empty."
    tags = [t.strip().lower() for t in (args.tag or []) if t.strip()]
    note = make_note(title, body, tags, getattr(args, "source_url",
None))
    if not note_is_valid(note):
        return "Error: validation failed."
    try:
        repo.save(note)
    except OSError as exc:
        return f"Error: failed to save note ({exc})."
    return f"Created: {format_note_preview(note)}"

def run_list_repo(repo: NoteRepository, args: argparse.Namespace) ->
str:
    notes = repo.list_all()
    limit = getattr(args, "limit", None)
    if limit is not None and limit <= 0:
        return "Error: limit must be positive."
    if limit is not None:
        notes = notes[:limit]
    if not notes:
        return "No notes found."
    return "\n".join(format_note_preview(n) for n in notes)

def run_search_repo(repo: NoteRepository, args: argparse.Namespace) -
> str:
    query = SearchQuery(
        text=getattr(args, "query", ""),
```

```
        tags=[t.strip().lower() for t in args.tag if t.strip()] if
getattr(args, "tag", None) else None,
        limit=getattr(args, "limit", None),
    )
    results = repo.search(query)
    if not results:
        return "No notes found."
    return "\n".join(format_note_preview(n) for n in results)

def run_export_repo(repo: NoteRepository, args: argparse.Namespace) -
> str:
    from compression.zstd import compress

    notes = repo.list_all()
    archive_path = getattr(args, "output", None)
    if archive_path is None:
        if repo.path is not None:
            archive_path = repo.path.with_suffix(".json.zst")
        else:
            archive_path = Path.home() / ".knowledge_tracker" /
"notes.json.zst"
    archive_path.parent.mkdir(parents=True, exist_ok=True)
    payload = json.dumps([n.to_dict() for n in notes], indent=2,
ensure_ascii=False).encode("utf-8")
    compressed = compress(payload)
    try:
        with archive_path.open("wb") as f:
            f.write(compressed)
    except OSError as exc:
        return f"Error: failed to write archive ({exc})."
    return f"Exported {len(notes)} notes to {archive_path}"
```

Each handler now depends on an abstraction. You can pass an `InMemoryNoteRepository` in tests and a `JsonNoteRepository` in production without changing any command logic.

Step 8: CLI Assembly

Wire the pieces together in a new entry point. Instantiate `JsonNoteRepository`, parse arguments, and dispatch.

```
def build_enhanced_parser() -> argparse.ArgumentParser:
    parser = argparse.ArgumentParser(prog="knowledge-tracker")
    subparsers = parser.add_subparsers(dest="command", required=True)

    create = subparsers.add_parser("create")
    create.add_argument("title")
    create.add_argument("body")
    create.add_argument("--tag", action="append", default=[])
```

```
    create.add_argument("--source-url", default=None)

    list_ = subparsers.add_parser("list")
    list_.add_argument("--limit", type=int, default=None)

    search = subparsers.add_parser("search")
    search.add_argument("query", nargs="?", default="")
    search.add_argument("--tag", action="append", default=[])
    search.add_argument("--limit", type=int, default=None)

    export = subparsers.add_parser("export")
    export.add_argument("output", nargs="?", type=Path, default=None)

    return parser

def run_enhanced_cli() -> None:
    args = build_enhanced_parser().parse_args()
    repo = JsonNoteRepository()

    match args.command:
        case "create":
            print(run_create_repo(repo, args))
        case "list":
            print(run_list_repo(repo, args))
        case "search":
            print(run_search_repo(repo, args))
        case "export":
            print(run_export_repo(repo, args))
        case _:
            print("Unknown command.")
```

The new CLI entry point is the only place that knows which repository implementation to create. Every layer beneath it works against the `NoteRepository` protocol.

Full Example

The following consolidated module places every type and function from the steps into a single runnable script. Here is the complete module.

Integrate the example into the tracker package as shown below. Place `NoteId`, `Tag`, `BaseEntity`, `Note`, `SearchQuery`, `_utc_now`, `_make_note_id`, `make_note`, `note_is_valid`, and `format_note_preview` in `models.py`. Place `NoteRepository`, `InMemoryNoteRepository`, and `JsonNoteRepository` in `storage.py`. Place `run_create_repo`, `run_list_repo`, `run_search_repo`, and `run_export_repo` in `commands.py`. Place `build_enhanced_parser` and `run_enhanced_cli` in `cli.py`.

```
# ch08_classes.py
import argparse
import json
from dataclasses import dataclass
from datetime import datetime, timezone
from pathlib import Path
from typing import Protocol, override

from compression.zstd import compress

type NoteId = str
type Tag = str

def _utc_now() -> str:
    return datetime.now(timezone.utc).isoformat()

def _make_note_id(title: str) -> NoteId:
    safe = "".join(c if c.isalnum() else "_" for c in title.lower())
    ts = datetime.now(timezone.utc).strftime("%Y%m%d%H%M%S%f")
    return f"note-{safe}-{ts}"

@dataclass
class BaseEntity:
    id: NoteId
    created: str

    def to_dict(self) -> dict[str, object]:
        return {"id": self.id, "created": self.created}

@dataclass
class Note(BaseEntity):
    title: str
    body: str
    tags: list[Tag]
    source_url: str | None = None

    @property
    def has_source(self) -> bool:
        return self.source_url is not None and
self.source_url.startswith(("http://", "https://"))

    @override
    def to_dict(self) -> dict[str, object]:
        base = super().to_dict()
        base.update({
            "title": self.title,
            "body": self.body,
            "tags": self.tags,
            "source_url": self.source_url,
        })
        return base

    def preview(self) -> str:
        tag_line = ", ".join(f"#{t}" for t in self.tags) if self.tags
```

```
else "no tags"
        return f"{self.title} [{tag_line}]"

@dataclass
class SearchQuery:
    text: str = ""
    tags: list[Tag] | None = None
    limit: int | None = None

def make_note(
    title: str,
    body: str,
    tags: list[Tag],
    source_url: str | None = None,
) -> Note:
    return Note(
        id=_make_note_id(title),
        created=_utc_now(),
        title=title,
        body=body,
        tags=[t.strip().lower() for t in tags if t.strip()],
        source_url=source_url,
    )

def note_is_valid(note: Note) -> bool:
    return bool(note.title.strip()) and bool(note.body.strip())

def format_note_preview(note: Note) -> str:
    return note.preview()

class NoteRepository(Protocol):
    path: Path | None

    def save(self, note: Note) -> None: ...
    def list_all(self) -> list[Note]: ...
    def search(self, query: SearchQuery) -> list[Note]: ...

class InMemoryNoteRepository:
    def __init__(self) -> None:
        self._notes: list[Note] = []
        self.path: Path | None = None

    def save(self, note: Note) -> None:
        self._notes.append(note)

    def list_all(self) -> list[Note]:
        return list(self._notes)

    def search(self, query: SearchQuery) -> list[Note]:
        results = self._notes
        if query.tags:
            results = [
                n for n in results
                if all(t.lower() in (tag.lower() for tag in n.tags)
```

```
for t in query.tags)
            ]
        if query.text:
            q = query.text.lower()
            results = [
                n for n in results
                if q in n.title.lower()
                or q in n.body.lower()
                or (n.source_url and q in n.source_url.lower())
            ]
        if query.limit is not None and query.limit > 0:
            results = results[:query.limit]
        return list(results)

class JsonNoteRepository(InMemoryNoteRepository):
    def __init__(self, path: Path | None = None) -> None:
        super().__init__()
        self._path = path or Path.home() / ".knowledge_tracker" /
"notes.json"
        self.path = self._path
        self._load()

    def _load(self) -> None:
        if not self._path.exists():
            return
        try:
            with self._path.open("r", encoding="utf-8") as f:
                data = json.load(f)
        except (json.JSONDecodeError, OSError):
            return
        if not isinstance(data, list):
            return
        for item in data:
            if not isinstance(item, dict):
                continue
            try:
                raw_tags = item.get("tags", [])
                tags: list[str] = []
                if isinstance(raw_tags, list):
                    tags = [
                        str(t).strip().lower()
                        for t in raw_tags
                        if isinstance(t, str) and str(t).strip()
                    ]
                note = Note(
                    id=str(item.get("id", "")),
                    created=str(item.get("created", "")),
                    title=str(item.get("title", "")),
                    body=str(item.get("body", "")),
                    tags=tags,
                    source_url=item.get("source_url") if
isinstance(item.get("source_url"), str) else None,
                )
                self._notes.append(note)
```

```
            except (TypeError, ValueError):
                continue

    @override
    def save(self, note: Note) -> None:
        super().save(note)
        self._persist()

    def _persist(self) -> None:
        self._path.parent.mkdir(parents=True, exist_ok=True)
        with self._path.open("w", encoding="utf-8") as f:
            json.dump([n.to_dict() for n in self._notes], f,
indent=2, ensure_ascii=False)

def run_create_repo(repo: NoteRepository, args: argparse.Namespace) -
> str:
    title = args.title.strip()
    body = args.body.strip()
    if not title or not body:
        return "Error: title and body cannot be empty."
    tags = [t.strip().lower() for t in (args.tag or []) if t.strip()]
    note = make_note(title, body, tags, getattr(args, "source_url",
None))
    if not note_is_valid(note):
        return "Error: validation failed."
    try:
        repo.save(note)
    except OSError as exc:
        return f"Error: failed to save note ({exc})."
    return f"Created: {format_note_preview(note)}"

def run_list_repo(repo: NoteRepository, args: argparse.Namespace) ->
str:
    notes = repo.list_all()
    limit = getattr(args, "limit", None)
    if limit is not None and limit <= 0:
        return "Error: limit must be positive."
    if limit is not None:
        notes = notes[:limit]
    if not notes:
        return "No notes found."
    return "\n".join(format_note_preview(n) for n in notes)

def run_search_repo(repo: NoteRepository, args: argparse.Namespace) -
> str:
    query = SearchQuery(
        text=getattr(args, "query", ""),
        tags=[t.strip().lower() for t in args.tag if t.strip()] if
getattr(args, "tag", None) else None,
        limit=getattr(args, "limit", None),
    )
    results = repo.search(query)
    if not results:
        return "No notes found."
```

```
    return "\n".join(format_note_preview(n) for n in results)

def run_export_repo(repo: NoteRepository, args: argparse.Namespace) -
> str:
    notes = repo.list_all()
    archive_path = getattr(args, "output", None)
    if archive_path is None:
        if repo.path is not None:
            archive_path = repo.path.with_suffix(".json.zst")
        else:
            archive_path = Path.home() / ".knowledge_tracker" /
"notes.json.zst"
    archive_path.parent.mkdir(parents=True, exist_ok=True)
    payload = json.dumps([n.to_dict() for n in notes], indent=2,
ensure_ascii=False).encode("utf-8")
    compressed = compress(payload)
    try:
        with archive_path.open("wb") as f:
            f.write(compressed)
    except OSError as exc:
        return f"Error: failed to write archive ({exc})."
    return f"Exported {len(notes)} notes to {archive_path}"

def build_enhanced_parser() -> argparse.ArgumentParser:
    parser = argparse.ArgumentParser(prog="knowledge-tracker")
    subparsers = parser.add_subparsers(dest="command", required=True)
    create = subparsers.add_parser("create")
    create.add_argument("title")
    create.add_argument("body")
    create.add_argument("--tag", action="append", default=[])
    create.add_argument("--source-url", default=None)
    list_ = subparsers.add_parser("list")
    list_.add_argument("--limit", type=int, default=None)
    search = subparsers.add_parser("search")
    search.add_argument("query", nargs="?", default="")
    search.add_argument("--tag", action="append", default=[])
    search.add_argument("--limit", type=int, default=None)
    export = subparsers.add_parser("export")
    export.add_argument("output", nargs="?", type=Path, default=None)
    return parser

def run_enhanced_cli() -> None:
    args = build_enhanced_parser().parse_args()
    repo = JsonNoteRepository()
    match args.command:
        case "create":
            print(run_create_repo(repo, args))
        case "list":
            print(run_list_repo(repo, args))
        case "search":
            print(run_search_repo(repo, args))
        case "export":
            print(run_export_repo(repo, args))
        case _:
```

```
            print("Unknown command.")

if __name__ == "__main__":
    run_enhanced_cli()
```

The script preserves the CLI contracts from Chapter 6 while replacing every internal data structure with typed models. `JsonNoteRepository` inherits search behavior from `InMemoryNoteRepository` and only overrides the persistence boundary. Command handlers stay pure: they receive a repository and an argument namespace.

Common Mistakes

- **Using mutable defaults in dataclass fields.** Writing `tags: list[Tag] = []` inside a `@dataclass` definition raises `ValueError` at class definition time. The check is narrow: `@dataclass` only rejects `list`, `dict`, and `set` literal defaults, detected because their type has `__hash__` set to `None`. It does not catch arbitrary mutable objects, such as an instance of a custom mutable class, so those slip through unguarded. For any mutable default, use `field(default_factory=...)` instead.

```
from dataclasses import dataclass, field

@dataclass
class Note:
    title: str
    tags: list[str] = field(default_factory=list)
```

- **Violating field ordering in inheritance.** Adding a required field after an optional field in a subclass triggers a `TypeError` at class definition time. Keep required fields before optional ones, and remember that inherited fields are ordered first.
- **Confusing `Protocol` with abstract base classes.** A `Protocol` does not require subclasses to inherit from it explicitly. Structural subtyping means any class with matching methods qualifies. Do not add unnecessary parent classes just to satisfy a protocol.
- **Forgetting `@override` on intentional method replacements.** Without it, a rename in the parent class leaves the subclass method

orphaned. The decorator turns that silent drift into a type-checking error.

- **Mixing dict access and attribute access during migration.** Code that previously used `note["title"]` must switch to `note.title` when moving to dataclasses. Mixed access patterns cause `TypeError` at runtime. Keep `NoteDict` helpers and `Note` helpers separate until the migration is complete.
- **Performing I/O inside the Protocol definition.** Protocols describe method signatures, not implementation. Never include concrete logic or field initialization inside a protocol body.

Performance and Production Considerations

- `@dataclass` generates `__init__` and `__eq__` at import time. The per-instance cost is identical to a hand-written class; there is no runtime decorator overhead after definition.
- `__eq__` compares every field recursively. For large or deeply nested models, equality checks can become expensive. Set `eq=False` on the dataclass if you do not need value-based equality.
- `InMemoryNoteRepository.search` builds intermediate lists for each filter stage. For the tracker's expected local dataset this is negligible, but for larger corpora, use generator-based pipelines or pre-built indexes as shown in Chapter 5.
- `JsonNoteRepository` rewrites the entire JSON file on every `save` call. This is simple and durable for a personal CLI tool, but it does not scale to high write throughput. If write volume grows, switch to append-only logs or SQLite.
- Protocols are enforced by static analysis, not at runtime. CPython does not validate that an object matches a protocol when you pass it to a function. Run `mypy` or `pyright` in CI to catch mismatches before deployment.
- The one-shot `compress` function inside `run_export_repo` returns a complete frame in a single call, which is ideal for the tracker's single-archive exports. For streaming large payloads in chunks, `ZstdCompressor` supports incremental `.compress()` calls followed by a

final `.flush()` to emit the frame tail; the tracker's single-archive exports do not need that complexity.

Summary

This chapter added typed `Note` and `SearchQuery` dataclasses alongside the existing dictionary-based helpers. You attached behavior through methods and properties, extended a `BaseEntity` parent, and used `@override` to make intent explicit. A `NoteRepository` protocol decoupled the new command handlers from storage details, enabling an in-memory implementation for tests and a JSON-backed implementation for production. The new `run_enhanced_cli` entry point is the only layer that knows which repository to instantiate. The result is a codebase that surfaces more errors during type checking, runs tests faster, and adapts to new storage backends without touching business logic.

Key Terms

- `@dataclass`: decorator that generates `__init__`, `__repr__`, and `__eq__` from declared fields
- `@property`: decorator that exposes a method as a read-only attribute without call syntax
- `@override`: decorator from `typing` that marks a method as intentionally replacing a parent method
- Protocol: type that defines an interface by method shape rather than explicit inheritance
- Structural subtyping: interface satisfaction determined by available methods and attributes, not by subclassing
- Repository pattern: abstraction that hides storage details behind a uniform interface
- Dependency inversion: designing components to depend on abstractions instead of concrete classes

Mini Quiz

1. **When defining a dataclass subclass such as `Note(BaseEntity)`, where must fields without defaults appear relative to fields with defaults?**

   A. After fields with defaults

   B. Before fields with defaults

   C. In any order if the base class uses `@dataclass(kw_only=True)`

   D. Only in the base class, never in the subclass

2. **The `JsonNoteRepository` class implements all methods required by `NoteRepository` but does not inherit from it. Which statement is true under static type checking when the instance is used where `NoteRepository` is expected?**

   A. mypy rejects it because explicit inheritance is mandatory for protocols

   B. CPython raises `TypeError` at runtime because the class lacks explicit inheritance

   C. It is a valid substitute because Python protocols use structural subtyping

   D. The protocol must be decorated with `@runtime_checkable` for mypy to accept it

3. **A developer renames `save` to `store` in `InMemoryNoteRepository` but leaves `@override` on `JsonNoteRepository.save`. What happens during type checking?**

   A. mypy reports an error because the overridden method no longer exists in the parent

   B. CPython raises a `RuntimeWarning` when the module is imported

   C. The decorator silently falls back to treating the method as a new definition

   D. `JsonNoteRepository` automatically inherits the renamed parent method

4. **Which definition safely provides an empty list default for a dataclass field `tags: list[Tag]` in the `Note` model?**

   A. `tags: list[Tag] = []`

B. `tags: list[Tag] = field(default=[])`

C. `tags: list[Tag] = field(default_factory=list)`

D. `tags: list[Tag] | None = None`

5. **Why do the tracker's command handlers accept the `NoteRepository` protocol instead of the concrete `JsonNoteRepository` class?**

   A. To avoid importing `json` inside the handler module

   B. To allow injecting `InMemoryNoteRepository` during tests without changing handler code

   C. Because protocols enforce runtime validation of method signatures

   D. Because `JsonNoteRepository` cannot be imported due to a circular dependency

Answers are provided in the Answer Key at the end of the book.

Activity

- Add a `delete(note_id: NoteId) -> bool` method to the `NoteRepository` protocol. It should return `True` when a note with the given ID exists and is removed, and `False` otherwise.
- Implement `delete` in `InMemoryNoteRepository` to scan `self._notes`, remove the first note whose `id` matches, and return whether a match was found.
- Override `delete` in `JsonNoteRepository` to delegate to the parent implementation and call `self._persist()` only when the parent returns `True`. Mark the override with `@override`.
- Add a new `remove` subcommand to `build_enhanced_parser` that accepts a positional `note_id` argument.
- Write a `run_remove(repo: NoteRepository, args: argparse.Namespace) -> str` handler that calls `repo.delete(args.note_id)` and returns `"Removed note {id}"` on success or `"Note not found"` otherwise.
- Register the `remove` case in the `match` block inside `run_enhanced_cli` so it prints the result of `run_remove`.
- Verify the behavior by running the tracker with the `create` subcommand twice and noting the returned note ID each time. Run `list` to confirm both notes appear. Run `remove` with one of the IDs you noted. Run `list` again to confirm the note is gone.

Chapter 9: Application Errors, Exceptions, and Logging

What You Will Learn

- Design a custom exception hierarchy that distinguishes validation, storage, and export failures in the Personal Knowledge Tracker CLI
- Use `try/except/else/finally` to handle errors at the appropriate architectural layer without silent failures
- Apply Python 3.14 bracketless `except` syntax for concise multi-exception handling (PEP 758)
- Chain exceptions with `raise ... from ...` to preserve debugging context across abstraction boundaries
- Configure the `logging` module for operational diagnostics instead of relying on `print()`
- Implement a top-level CLI exception boundary that logs internal details and prints friendly user messages

Prerequisites

- Completion of Chapter 8 (Classes, Dataclasses, and Protocols): `@dataclass` models (`Note`, `SearchQuery`), `NoteRepository` protocol, `JsonNoteRepository`, `make_note`, `note_is_valid`, `format_note_preview`, and `build_enhanced_parser`
- Completion of Chapter 6 (Files, Paths, I/O): `pathlib.Path`, JSON serialization, `compression.zstd`, and `OSError` from file operations
- Completion of Chapter 3 (Control Flow): `argparse` subparsers and `argparse.Namespace`
- Completion of Chapter 4 (Functions): typed signatures, keyword-only arguments, and mutable-default safety

Concept Overview

Ad-hoc error handling breaks down the moment a CLI grows beyond toy size. Returning error strings from deep inside a call stack forces every intermediate layer to forward that string, and `print()` calls buried in library code destroy the separation between user interface and operational diagnostics. Structured exceptions solve both problems. Each architectural layer decides whether to recover, translate, or escalate. Distinct exception types let callers branch programmatically.

When Python raises an exception, the runtime unwinds the call stack until it finds a matching `except` clause. If none is found, the program terminates with a traceback. Catching stops propagation. Re-raising with `raise ... from ...` preserves the original context while attaching new domain meaning. Unhandled exceptions propagate upward by default, which is why a top-level boundary is essential.

Python 3.14 adds bracketless `except` clauses (PEP 758). You can omit the parentheses when catching multiple exception types, but only when you do not bind the caught exception. `except ValueError, TypeError:` is legal. When you need the bound name with `as e`, parentheses are still required: `except (ValueError, TypeError) as e:`. The form `except ValueError, TypeError as e:` is a `SyntaxError`. This removes visual noise when you want to handle several related failures the same way.

Replace `print()` with the `logging` module for operational output. Log records carry timestamps, severity levels, and source names. They can be filtered, formatted, and routed to files or streams without changing application code.

User-facing messages belong in the CLI layer. Diagnostic details belong in the log.

Resilience requires clear boundaries. The Personal Knowledge Tracker CLI now crosses a reliability threshold. Missing files, malformed JSON, permission errors, and invalid user input must each be caught, logged, and reported without crashing the process. A single top-level boundary catches domain errors and prints concise messages. The log stream keeps the stack traces.

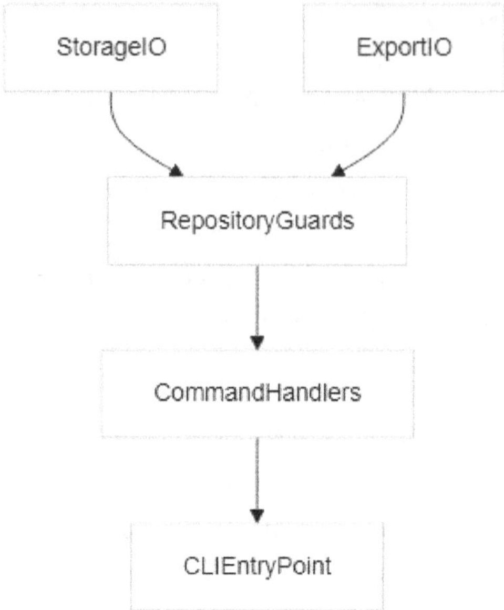

Step-by-Step Implementation

Step 1: Define a Domain Exception Hierarchy

Start with a single base exception that identifies every error originating inside the tracker. Derive specific subclasses for validation, storage, and export failures. This lets the CLI boundary catch `TrackerError` broadly while allowing intermediate code to react to specific types.

```
# src/knowledge_tracker/exceptions.py

class TrackerError(Exception):
    """Base exception for all Personal Knowledge Tracker errors."""
    pass

class NoteValidationError(TrackerError):
    """Raised when note data fails domain validation."""
    pass

class StorageError(TrackerError):
    """Raised when reading or writing persisted note data fails."""
    pass

class ExportError(TrackerError):
    """Raised when compressing or writing an export archive fails."""
    pass
```

Inheritance matters. Catching `TrackerError` at the top level traps every domain-specific problem without masking unrelated bugs like `NameError` or `AttributeError`.

Keep the hierarchy shallow. Deep exception trees create classification fatigue.

Step 2: Configure Operational Logging

Create a small configuration function that sets up a stream handler, a formatter, and the root logger level. Call this once at application startup.

```
# src/knowledge_tracker/logging_config.py
import logging
import sys

def configure_logging(level: int = logging.INFO) -> None:
    handler = logging.StreamHandler(sys.stderr)
    formatter = logging.Formatter(
        "%(asctime)s [%(levelname)s] %(name)s: %(message)s",
        datefmt="%Y-%m-%d %H:%M:%S",
    )
    handler.setFormatter(formatter)
    root = logging.getLogger()
    root.setLevel(level)
    if not root.handlers:
        root.addHandler(handler)
```

Loggers are hierarchical. Use `logging.getLogger(__name__)` in each module so log records identify their source.

Avoid the root logger inside library modules.

The function adds a handler only if the root logger has none, making it safe to call multiple times.

Step 3: Validate with Exceptions Instead of Booleans

Replace boolean validation checks with guard functions that raise `NoteValidationError` on failure. This pushes error handling to the caller and eliminates the risk of ignoring a `False` return value.

```
# src/knowledge_tracker/validators.py
from knowledge_tracker.models import Note, note_is_valid
from knowledge_tracker.exceptions import NoteValidationError
```

```
def ensure_valid_note(note: Note) -> None:
    if not note_is_valid(note):
        raise NoteValidationError(
            f"Note failed validation: title={note.title!r},
body={note.body!r}"
        )
```

The caller must now deal with the failure. There is no silent path where an invalid note slips through because someone forgot to check a return value.

Step 4: Translate Low-Level I/O Failures

Repository operations raise `OSError` when disks fill up, permissions deny access, or files vanish. Wrap those operations in guards that catch `OSError` and re-raise `StorageError` with exception chaining. Chaining preserves the original traceback while attaching domain context.

These guards protect operations on an existing repository instance. Repository initialization is guarded separately at the CLI boundary.

```
# src/knowledge_tracker/storage.py
# ... existing NoteRepository, InMemoryNoteRepository,
JsonNoteRepository ...
from knowledge_tracker.models import Note, SearchQuery
from knowledge_tracker.exceptions import StorageError

def load_notes_guarded(repo: NoteRepository) -> list[Note]:
    try:
        return repo.list_all()
    except (OSError, ValueError, TypeError) as exc:
        path = repo.path if repo.path else "<memory>"
        raise StorageError(f"Failed to load notes from {path}:
{exc}") from exc

def save_notes_guarded(repo: NoteRepository, note: Note) -> None:
    try:
        repo.save(note)
    except OSError as exc:
        path = repo.path if repo.path else "<memory>"
        raise StorageError(f"Failed to save note to {path}") from exc

def search_notes_guarded(repo: NoteRepository, query: SearchQuery) ->
list[Note]:
    try:
        return repo.search(query)
    except OSError as exc:
        raise StorageError(f"Search failed: {exc}") from exc
```

The `raise ... from ...` syntax links the new `StorageError` to the original `OSError`. Without `from`, the original exception is still reachable via `__context__`, but the causal chain is implicit. Explicit chaining produces clearer tracebacks and documents the intent to translate the error. Never hide the cause.

Catching `ValueError` and `TypeError` alongside `OSError` in `load_notes_guarded` defends against malformed persisted note data that survives JSON parsing but fails `Note` reconstruction.

Step 5: Translate Export Failures

Exporting involves both JSON serialization and Zstandard compression. Isolate those steps behind a guard that raises `ExportError`.

```
# src/knowledge_tracker/export.py
import json
from pathlib import Path
from compression.zstd import compress

from knowledge_tracker.models import Note
from knowledge_tracker.exceptions import ExportError

def export_archive_guarded(notes: list[Note], archive_path: Path) ->
None:
    try:
        archive_path.parent.mkdir(parents=True, exist_ok=True)
        payload = json.dumps(
            [n.to_dict() for n in notes],
            indent=2,
            ensure_ascii=False,
        ).encode("utf-8")
        compressed = compress(payload)
        with archive_path.open("wb") as f:
            f.write(compressed)
    except (OSError, TypeError) as exc:
        raise ExportError(f"Failed to export archive to
{archive_path}") from exc
```

Catching `TypeError` alongside `OSError` defends against unexpected serialization or compression edge cases. Translate them all into the domain exception so the CLI boundary handles them uniformly.

Step 6: Evolve Command Handlers with Error Handling and Logging

Refactor the command handlers from Chapter 8 to use the new guards, raise domain exceptions on invalid input, and emit log records at key events. Each handler requests its own module logger.

Step 6a: Refactor the Create Handler

The create handler validates input, builds the note, delegates validation to `ensure_valid_note`, persists through the guard, and logs the result.

```
# src/knowledge_tracker/commands.py
import argparse
import logging
from pathlib import Path

from knowledge_tracker.models import make_note, SearchQuery,
format_note_preview
from knowledge_tracker.storage import (
    NoteRepository,
    load_notes_guarded,
    save_notes_guarded,
    search_notes_guarded,
)
from knowledge_tracker.exceptions import NoteValidationError
from knowledge_tracker.export import export_archive_guarded
from knowledge_tracker.validators import ensure_valid_note

logger = logging.getLogger(__name__)

def run_create_logged(repo: NoteRepository, args: argparse.Namespace)
-> str:
    title = args.title.strip()
    body = args.body.strip()
    if not title or not body:
        raise NoteValidationError("Title and body cannot be blank.")
    tags = [t.strip().lower() for t in (args.tag or []) if t.strip()]
    note = make_note(title, body, tags, getattr(args, "source_url",
None))
    ensure_valid_note(note)
    save_notes_guarded(repo, note)
    logger.info("Created note %s", note.id)
    return f"Created note: {format_note_preview(note)}"
```

Step 6b: Refactor the Remaining Handlers

The list, search, and export handlers follow the same pattern: validate arguments, call guarded storage operations, and log outcomes.

```
def run_list_logged(repo: NoteRepository, args: argparse.Namespace) -
> str:
    limit = getattr(args, "limit", None)
    if limit is not None and limit <= 0:
        raise NoteValidationError("Limit must be a positive
integer.")
    notes = load_notes_guarded(repo)
    if limit is not None:
        notes = notes[:limit]
    if not notes:
        return "No notes found."
    logger.info("Listed %d notes", len(notes))
    return "\n".join(format_note_preview(n) for n in notes)

def run_search_logged(repo: NoteRepository, args: argparse.Namespace)
-> str:
    query = SearchQuery(
        text=getattr(args, "query", ""),
        tags=[t.strip().lower() for t in (args.tag or []) if
t.strip()] or None,
        limit=getattr(args, "limit", None),
    )
    results = search_notes_guarded(repo, query)
    if not results:
        return "No notes found."
    logger.info("Search returned %d results", len(results))
    return "\n".join(format_note_preview(n) for n in results)

def run_export_logged(repo: NoteRepository, args: argparse.Namespace)
-> str:
    notes = load_notes_guarded(repo)
    output = getattr(args, "output", None)
    if output:
        archive_path = Path(output)
    else:
        fallback = Path.home() / ".knowledge_tracker" / "notes.json"
        archive_path = (repo.path or
fallback).with_suffix(".json.zst")
    export_archive_guarded(notes, archive_path)
    logger.info("Exported %d notes to %s", len(notes), archive_path)
    return f"Exported {len(notes)} notes to {archive_path}"
```

The handlers return strings for the CLI to print; they never call `print()` themselves.

Validation errors raise immediately. I/O errors translate through the guards. Success paths log at `INFO` level.

Step 7: Demonstrate Python 3.14 Bracketless Except

PEP 758 lets you drop the parentheses when catching multiple exception types, as long as you do not bind the result with `as`. When you do need `as e`, the parentheses come back. The syntax is cleaner and reads like a list.

```
# src/knowledge_tracker/demo_syntax.py
from knowledge_tracker.exceptions import NoteValidationError,
StorageError

def demo_bracketless_except() -> None:
    for exc_cls in (NoteValidationError, StorageError, ValueError):
        try:
            raise exc_cls("demo error")
        except (NoteValidationError, StorageError) as e:
            print(f"Caught tracker error: {e}")
        except ValueError as e:
            print(f"Caught value error: {e}")
```

PEP 758 lets you drop the parentheses only when there is no `as` binding, as in `except NoteValidationError, StorageError:`. The moment you bind the caught exception with `as e`, parentheses are required again: `except (NoteValidationError, StorageError) as e:`, used above, is the legal form. Writing `except NoteValidationError, StorageError as e:` is a `SyntaxError`. The `as e` binds to whichever exception was caught.

When several operations fail at once, Python can raise an `ExceptionGroup` that bundles multiple exceptions together. The `except*` clause catches selected types out of that group while letting the rest propagate. This is how `asyncio.TaskGroup`, previewed in the asyncio chapter, surfaces concurrent failures, and the same PEP 758 bracketless rule applies: parenthesize the tuple whenever you bind with `as`.

The `print()` calls here are only for demonstration; production code would route output through the CLI layer.

Step 8: Wire the Resilient CLI Entry Point

The top-level runner configures logging, instantiates the repository, dispatches commands, and catches exceptions. Domain errors print friendly messages and send stack traces to the log. Unexpected errors receive a generic message. The user never sees internal filenames.

```
# src/knowledge_tracker/cli.py
import argparse
import logging
import sys

from knowledge_tracker.logging_config import configure_logging
from knowledge_tracker.storage import JsonNoteRepository
from knowledge_tracker.commands import (
    run_create_logged,
    run_list_logged,
    run_search_logged,
    run_export_logged,
)
from knowledge_tracker.exceptions import TrackerError, StorageError

def build_enhanced_parser() -> argparse.ArgumentParser:
    parser = argparse.ArgumentParser(prog="knowledge-tracker")
    subparsers = parser.add_subparsers(dest="command", required=True)

    create = subparsers.add_parser("create")
    create.add_argument("title")
    create.add_argument("body")
    create.add_argument("--tag", action="append", default=[])
    create.add_argument("--source-url", default=None)

    list_ = subparsers.add_parser("list")
    list_.add_argument("--limit", type=int, default=None)

    search = subparsers.add_parser("search")
    search.add_argument("query", nargs="?", default="")
    search.add_argument("--tag", action="append", default=[])
    search.add_argument("--limit", type=int, default=None)

    export = subparsers.add_parser("export")
    export.add_argument("--output", default=None)

    return parser

def run_resilient_cli() -> None:
    configure_logging(logging.INFO)
    logger = logging.getLogger(__name__)
    parser = build_enhanced_parser()
    args = parser.parse_args()

    try:
        try:
            repo = JsonNoteRepository()
        except OSError as exc:
            raise StorageError("Failed to initialize note storage")
from exc
```

```
        if args.command == "create":
            result = run_create_logged(repo, args)
        elif args.command == "list":
            result = run_list_logged(repo, args)
        elif args.command == "search":
            result = run_search_logged(repo, args)
        elif args.command == "export":
            result = run_export_logged(repo, args)
        else:
            result = "Unknown command."
        print(result)
    except TrackerError as exc:
        logger.exception("Command '%s' failed", args.command)
        print(f"Error: {exc}", file=sys.stderr)
        sys.exit(1)
    except Exception:
        logger.exception("Unexpected failure in command '%s'",
args.command)
        print("An unexpected error occurred. See logs for details.",
file=sys.stderr)
        sys.exit(1)
    else:
        logger.info("Command '%s' completed successfully",
args.command)
    finally:
        logger.debug("CLI dispatch finished")
```

The inner `try` block translates repository initialization errors into `StorageError` so the outer `TrackerError` boundary handles them uniformly. The outer boundary catches every domain problem we defined. `Exception` is a safety net for truly unexpected bugs. Both paths log the full exception before emitting a short user-facing message. The `else` clause logs success only when no exception occurs, and `finally` guarantees a completion record.

Full Example

The following files build on the Chapter 8 project. Place them into `src/knowledge_tracker/` alongside the existing models, storage, and CLI modules.

```
# src/knowledge_tracker/exceptions.py
class TrackerError(Exception):
    """Base exception for all Personal Knowledge Tracker errors."""
    pass

class NoteValidationError(TrackerError):
```

```
    """Raised when note data fails domain validation."""
    pass

class StorageError(TrackerError):
    """Raised when reading or writing persisted note data fails."""
    pass

class ExportError(TrackerError):
    """Raised when compressing or writing an export archive fails."""
    pass
```

```
# src/knowledge_tracker/logging_config.py
import logging
import sys

def configure_logging(level: int = logging.INFO) -> None:
    handler = logging.StreamHandler(sys.stderr)
    formatter = logging.Formatter(
        "%(asctime)s [%(levelname)s] %(name)s: %(message)s",
        datefmt="%Y-%m-%d %H:%M:%S",
    )
    handler.setFormatter(formatter)
    root = logging.getLogger()
    root.setLevel(level)
    if not root.handlers:
        root.addHandler(handler)
```

```
# src/knowledge_tracker/validators.py
from knowledge_tracker.models import Note, note_is_valid
from knowledge_tracker.exceptions import NoteValidationError

def ensure_valid_note(note: Note) -> None:
    if not note_is_valid(note):
        raise NoteValidationError(
            f"Note failed validation: title={note.title!r},
body={note.body!r}"
        )
```

```
# src/knowledge_tracker/storage.py
# ... existing NoteRepository, InMemoryNoteRepository,
JsonNoteRepository ...
from knowledge_tracker.models import Note, SearchQuery
from knowledge_tracker.exceptions import StorageError

def load_notes_guarded(repo: NoteRepository) -> list[Note]:
    try:
        return repo.list_all()
    except (OSError, ValueError, TypeError) as exc:
        path = repo.path if repo.path else "<memory>"
```

```
        raise StorageError(f"Failed to load notes from {path}:
{exc}") from exc

def save_notes_guarded(repo: NoteRepository, note: Note) -> None:
    try:
        repo.save(note)
    except OSError as exc:
        path = repo.path if repo.path else "<memory>"
        raise StorageError(f"Failed to save note to {path}") from exc

def search_notes_guarded(repo: NoteRepository, query: SearchQuery) ->
list[Note]:
    try:
        return repo.search(query)
    except OSError as exc:
        raise StorageError(f"Search failed: {exc}") from exc
```

```
# src/knowledge_tracker/export.py
import json
from pathlib import Path
from compression.zstd import compress

from knowledge_tracker.models import Note
from knowledge_tracker.exceptions import ExportError

def export_archive_guarded(notes: list[Note], archive_path: Path) ->
None:
    try:
        archive_path.parent.mkdir(parents=True, exist_ok=True)
        payload = json.dumps(
            [n.to_dict() for n in notes],
            indent=2,
            ensure_ascii=False,
        ).encode("utf-8")
        compressed = compress(payload)
        with archive_path.open("wb") as f:
            f.write(compressed)
    except (OSError, TypeError) as exc:
        raise ExportError(f"Failed to export archive to
{archive_path}") from exc
```

```
# src/knowledge_tracker/commands.py
import argparse
import logging
from pathlib import Path

from knowledge_tracker.models import make_note, SearchQuery,
format_note_preview
from knowledge_tracker.storage import (
    NoteRepository,
    load_notes_guarded,
```

```
    save_notes_guarded,
    search_notes_guarded,
)
from knowledge_tracker.exceptions import NoteValidationError
from knowledge_tracker.export import export_archive_guarded
from knowledge_tracker.validators import ensure_valid_note

logger = logging.getLogger(__name__)

def run_create_logged(repo: NoteRepository, args: argparse.Namespace)
-> str:
    title = args.title.strip()
    body = args.body.strip()
    if not title or not body:
        raise NoteValidationError("Title and body cannot be blank.")
    tags = [t.strip().lower() for t in (args.tag or []) if t.strip()]
    note = make_note(title, body, tags, getattr(args, "source_url",
None))
    ensure_valid_note(note)
    save_notes_guarded(repo, note)
    logger.info("Created note %s", note.id)
    return f"Created note: {format_note_preview(note)}"

def run_list_logged(repo: NoteRepository, args: argparse.Namespace) -
> str:
    limit = getattr(args, "limit", None)
    if limit is not None and limit <= 0:
        raise NoteValidationError("Limit must be a positive
integer.")
    notes = load_notes_guarded(repo)
    if limit is not None:
        notes = notes[:limit]
    if not notes:
        return "No notes found."
    logger.info("Listed %d notes", len(notes))
    return "\n".join(format_note_preview(n) for n in notes)

def run_search_logged(repo: NoteRepository, args: argparse.Namespace)
-> str:
    query = SearchQuery(
        text=getattr(args, "query", ""),
        tags=[t.strip().lower() for t in (args.tag or []) if
t.strip()] or None,
        limit=getattr(args, "limit", None),
    )
    results = search_notes_guarded(repo, query)
    if not results:
        return "No notes found."
    logger.info("Search returned %d results", len(results))
    return "\n".join(format_note_preview(n) for n in results)

def run_export_logged(repo: NoteRepository, args: argparse.Namespace)
-> str:
    notes = load_notes_guarded(repo)
```

```
    output = getattr(args, "output", None)
    if output:
        archive_path = Path(output)
    else:
        fallback = Path.home() / ".knowledge_tracker" / "notes.json"
        archive_path = (repo.path or
fallback).with_suffix(".json.zst")
    export_archive_guarded(notes, archive_path)
    logger.info("Exported %d notes to %s", len(notes), archive_path)
    return f"Exported {len(notes)} notes to {archive_path}"
```

```
# src/knowledge_tracker/demo_syntax.py
from knowledge_tracker.exceptions import NoteValidationError,
StorageError

def demo_bracketless_except() -> None:
    for exc_cls in (NoteValidationError, StorageError, ValueError):
        try:
            raise exc_cls("demo error")
        except (NoteValidationError, StorageError) as e:
            print(f"Caught tracker error: {e}")
        except ValueError as e:
            print(f"Caught value error: {e}")
```

```
# src/knowledge_tracker/cli.py
import argparse
import logging
import sys

from knowledge_tracker.logging_config import configure_logging
from knowledge_tracker.storage import JsonNoteRepository
from knowledge_tracker.commands import (
    run_create_logged,
    run_list_logged,
    run_search_logged,
    run_export_logged,
)
from knowledge_tracker.exceptions import TrackerError, StorageError

def build_enhanced_parser() -> argparse.ArgumentParser:
    parser = argparse.ArgumentParser(prog="knowledge-tracker")
    subparsers = parser.add_subparsers(dest="command", required=True)

    create = subparsers.add_parser("create")
    create.add_argument("title")
    create.add_argument("body")
    create.add_argument("--tag", action="append", default=[])
    create.add_argument("--source-url", default=None)

    list_ = subparsers.add_parser("list")
    list_.add_argument("--limit", type=int, default=None)
```

```
    search = subparsers.add_parser("search")
    search.add_argument("query", nargs="?", default="")
    search.add_argument("--tag", action="append", default=[])
    search.add_argument("--limit", type=int, default=None)

    export = subparsers.add_parser("export")
    export.add_argument("--output", default=None)

    return parser

def run_resilient_cli() -> None:
    configure_logging(logging.INFO)
    logger = logging.getLogger(__name__)
    parser = build_enhanced_parser()
    args = parser.parse_args()

    try:
        try:
            repo = JsonNoteRepository()
        except OSError as exc:
            raise StorageError("Failed to initialize note storage")
from exc

        if args.command == "create":
            result = run_create_logged(repo, args)
        elif args.command == "list":
            result = run_list_logged(repo, args)
        elif args.command == "search":
            result = run_search_logged(repo, args)
        elif args.command == "export":
            result = run_export_logged(repo, args)
        else:
            result = "Unknown command."
        print(result)
    except TrackerError as exc:
        logger.exception("Command '%s' failed", args.command)
        print(f"Error: {exc}", file=sys.stderr)
        sys.exit(1)
    except Exception:
        logger.exception("Unexpected failure in command '%s'",
args.command)
        print("An unexpected error occurred. See logs for details.",
file=sys.stderr)
        sys.exit(1)
    else:
        logger.info("Command '%s' completed successfully",
args.command)
    finally:
        logger.debug("CLI dispatch finished")
```

The architecture now has clear layers. `exceptions.py` owns the taxonomy of failures. `logging_config.py` owns diagnostics setup. `validators.py` and `storage.py` raise domain errors early. `commands.py` logs business events and lets exceptions propagate. `cli.py` owns the final boundary between internal detail and user experience.

Common Mistakes

- **Catching `Exception` too early.** Wrapping every function body in `except Exception` masks bugs and makes debugging painful. Catch specific exceptions at the layer where you can meaningfully respond; let everything else propagate.
- **Using `print()` for operational diagnostics.** `print()` bypasses severity levels, formatting, and redirection. Use `logging.debug`, `logging.info`, and `logging.error` so operators can tune verbosity without code changes.
- **Losing the original traceback.** Re-raising a new exception without `from` severs the explicit causal chain. Always use `raise StorageError(...) from exc` when translating low-level errors into domain exceptions.
- **Returning error strings instead of raising.** Functions that return `"Error: something failed"` force every caller to check for that sentinel. Exceptions are Python's native mechanism for unreachable return values. Use them.
- **Logging sensitive user data.** Never log raw exception messages that contain file paths, tokens, or note bodies in production. Scrub or parameterize log records when personal data is involved.
- **Forgetting to configure logging before the first log record.** An unconfigured logger drops records or uses a last-resort handler. Call `configure_logging` before any substantive work, ideally as the first statement in `run_resilient_cli`.

I once spent an hour debugging a tracker-like tool that swallowed a `PermissionError` because an earlier developer caught `OSError` and returned `None`. The application appeared to work; it just had no data. Raise exceptions. Return values demand discipline that code review cannot reliably enforce.

Performance and Production Considerations

Exception handling in CPython is fast when exceptions are rare. Do not use exceptions for control flow inside tight loops; reserve them for truly exceptional conditions. The tracker CLI is I/O bound, so the cost of raising during a failed file open is negligible compared to the syscall overhead.

Log formatting happens on the emitting thread. Heavy log volume can block the event loop in async contexts or slow down synchronous pipelines. For the tracker CLI, `StreamHandler` on `sys.stderr` is sufficient. If log volume grows, switch to `QueueHandler` with a background thread.

On a previous project, unbounded `StreamHandler` logging inside a tight ETL loop added fifteen percent overhead. Switching to `QueueHandler` dropped that to under one percent.

The one-shot `compress()` in `export_archive_guarded` returns a complete zstd frame in a single call, which is ideal for typical exports. For very large note collections, holding the full payload and its compressed output in memory at once creates memory pressure. When exports exceed a few megabytes, switch to the incremental `ZstdCompressor`, feeding the input in chunks with repeated `.compress()` calls and a final `.flush()` to close the frame.

Commit `uv.lock` and pin dependency hashes. A runtime failure caused by a changed transitive dependency is harder to diagnose than a build failure. Lockfiles prevent that class of error.

Summary

Ad-hoc error strings are now gone from the Personal Knowledge Tracker CLI. A structured exception hierarchy classifies every failure mode. You defined `TrackerError`, `NoteValidationError`, `StorageError`, and `ExportError` to separate validation, storage, and export problems. `try/except/else/finally` and `raise ... from ...` translate low-level `OSError` instances into domain exceptions without losing context. Python 3.14 bracketless `except` syntax cleans up multi-catch clauses. The `logging` module now handles operational diagnostics; `print()` remains reserved for user-facing CLI output. A resilient boundary around the command dispatch loop logs stack traces, prints concise error messages, and uses `else` and `finally` for success and completion bookkeeping.

The result is a CLI that fails safely. Invalid input produces clear guidance. Disk errors produce actionable logs. Unexpected bugs stay internal. That is the baseline for production Python tooling.

Key Terms

- **TrackerError**: Base exception class for all domain-specific errors in the Personal Knowledge Tracker CLI.
- **NoteValidationError**: Exception subclass raised when note data fails domain validation rules.
- **StorageError**: Exception subclass raised when reading or writing persisted note data fails.
- **ExportError**: Exception subclass raised when compressing or writing a Zstandard export archive fails.
- **Exception chaining**: Linking a new exception to an original exception using `raise ... from ...` so the causal chain and traceback remain intact for debugging.
- **Bracketless except**: Python 3.14 syntax (PEP 758) that allows multiple exception types in a single `except` clause without parentheses.
- **Exception boundary**: A top-level catch block that separates internal error details from user-facing messages.
- **Operational logging**: Diagnostic output using the `logging` module instead of `print()` to gain severity levels, timestamps, and configurable redirection.

Mini Quiz

1. **A user runs** `knowledge-tracker create --title "Tip" --body "Details"` **and the disk is full.** `JsonNoteRepository.save` **raises** `OSError`**, which** `save_notes_guarded` **translates into** `StorageError`**. What does the user see on stderr?**

   A. A full Python traceback ending in `OSError: [Errno 28] No space left on device`

   B. `Error: Could not open note storage.`

   C. `Error: Failed to save note to /home/user/.knowledge_tracker/notes.json`

   D. Nothing; the process exits with code 0 and no output

2. **Consider this snippet:**

```
try:
    repo = JsonNoteRepository()
except OSError as exc:
    raise StorageError("Initialization failed") from exc
```

What is the primary benefit of `from exc`?

   A. It suppresses the original `OSError` so only `StorageError` appears in logs.

   B. It automatically retries the failed operation once before crashing.

   C. It preserves the original traceback and causal chain for debugging.

   D. It converts the exception into a non-fatal warning.

3. **Why should** `print()` **be avoided for operational diagnostics in production CLI tools?**

   A. `print()` writes to stdout, which is slower than stderr.

   B. `print()` lacks severity levels, timestamps, and configurable redirection.

   C. `print()` raises `BufferError` when the terminal buffer fills.

   D. `print()` is deprecated in Python 3.14 and will be removed.

4. **Which form correctly catches both** `NoteValidationError` **and** `StorageError` **in a single clause and binds the caught exception to** `e` **in Python 3.14?**

A. `except (NoteValidationError, StorageError) as e:`

B. `except NoteValidationError, StorageError as e:`

C. `except NoteValidationError | StorageError as e:`

D. `except [NoteValidationError, StorageError] as e:`

5. **In `run_resilient_cli`, why is `TrackerError` caught before the bare `Exception` handler?**

   A. To ensure domain errors receive a specific user-facing message while unexpected bugs receive a generic one.

   B. Because `TrackerError` is not a subclass of `Exception` in Python 3.14.

   C. Because catching `Exception` first would raise a `SyntaxError`.

   D. To prevent domain errors from being written to the log file.

Answers are provided in the Answer Key at the end of the book.

Activity

Extend the Personal Knowledge Tracker CLI with a bulk import command that exercises custom exceptions, exception chaining, bracketless except syntax, and operational logging.

- Add `NoteImportError(TrackerError)` to `src/knowledge_tracker/exceptions.py`.
- Create `run_import_logged(repo, args)` in `src/knowledge_tracker/commands.py` that reads a JSON file path from `args.source`.
- Inside `run_import_logged`, open the source file with `pathlib.Path` and load the JSON payload. Use a `try` block to catch `OSError` and `json.JSONDecodeError`. Because you need the bound name to chain with `from`, parenthesize the tuple: `except (OSError, json.JSONDecodeError) as exc:`, then raise `NoteImportError(...) from exc` to preserve the original traceback.
- Verify the loaded JSON is a list. Iterate over each item. If an item is not a dictionary or lacks required fields, log a warning and skip it.
- For each valid dictionary, construct a `Note` using `make_note`. Call `ensure_valid_note` on the result inside a `try` block. If it raises `NoteValidationError`, log a warning and skip the item.
- Save each valid note using `save_notes_guarded` so disk errors are translated into `StorageError` automatically.
- After processing all items, log an `INFO` record stating how many notes were imported and return a success string.
- Register a new `import` subcommand in `build_enhanced_parser` that takes a positional `source` argument.
- Wire the `import` branch inside `run_resilient_cli` so it calls `run_import_logged` and routes any `TrackerError` through the existing exception boundary.
- Test the command by creating a JSON file with a mix of valid note dictionaries and malformed entries. Verify that valid notes are persisted, invalid entries produce warnings, and missing files produce a friendly error message on stderr.

Part IV: Production Practice

Chapter 10: Async I/O and Concurrency Choices

What You Will Learn

- Write coroutines with `async` and `await` and execute them using `asyncio.run()`
- Use `asyncio.TaskGroup` to manage concurrent async tasks with automatic cancellation
- Integrate async HTTP requests via `httpx` into the Personal Knowledge Tracker CLI to fetch URL metadata
- Select appropriate concurrency models for different workloads: async I/O for network bounds, threading for concurrent I/O, free-threaded Python for CPU parallelism, multiprocessing for process isolation, and subinterpreters for in-process isolation
- Detect whether the current interpreter runs with the GIL enabled using `sys._is_gil_enabled()`

Prerequisites

- Completion of Chapter 8 (classes, dataclasses, protocols, and the `NoteRepository` boundary)
- Completion of Chapter 9 (custom exceptions, logging, and guarded storage functions)
- Familiarity with `pathlib`, JSON persistence, and `argparse` subparsers from Chapters 6 and 7

Concept Overview

Python offers several concurrency models. Choosing the wrong one produces sluggish performance, wasted memory, or fragile code. This chapter teaches structured async I/O by adding metadata fetching to the Personal Knowledge Tracker CLI. When a note includes a source URL, the tracker fetches the remote page title and description asynchronously. For this chapter, fetched metadata is displayed in the CLI summary; persisting it back into the note record is left as a future extension.

Async I/O runs on a single thread, scheduled cooperatively by an event loop. When a coroutine awaits a network response, the loop switches to another ready task. This model excels at high-concurrency network work because it avoids the memory overhead of thousands of OS threads. I once debugged a production pipeline that lost forty percent of its throughput because engineers dropped synchronous `requests` calls inside `asyncio` coroutines; switching to `httpx.AsyncClient` restored the concurrency budget immediately.

The `async` keyword declares a coroutine function. The `await` keyword yields control back to the event loop until the awaited operation completes. `asyncio.run()` is the canonical entry point for async programs. It creates an event loop, runs the passed coroutine to completion, and closes the loop.

Python 3.11 introduced `asyncio.TaskGroup`. It provides structured concurrency. Tasks spawned inside a TaskGroup run concurrently. If any task raises an exception, the group cancels the remaining tasks and raises an `ExceptionGroup`. No task is left orphaned.

Async I/O is the wrong abstraction for CPU-bound work. The standard CPython build retains the Global Interpreter Lock (GIL), so Python threads do not execute bytecode in parallel. Python 3.14 ships an opt-in free-threaded build, `python3.14t`, which removes the GIL and allows true thread-level parallelism. Multiprocessing sidesteps the GIL entirely by spawning separate OS processes. Python 3.14 also introduces `concurrent.interpreters`, which creates isolated interpreter contexts inside a single process. Each subinterpreter has its own GIL and module state.

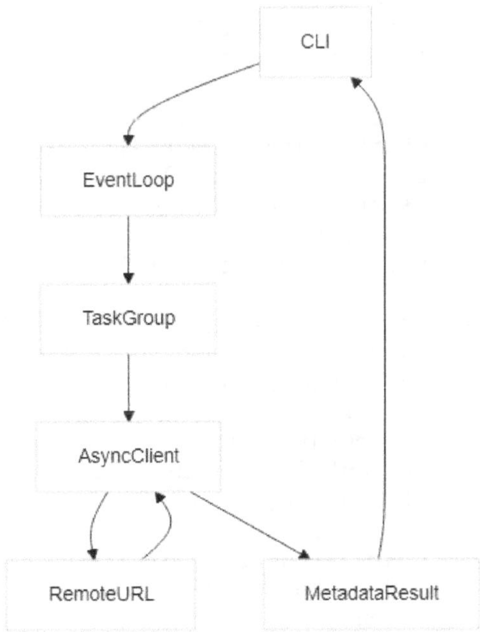

Step-by-Step Implementation

Step 1: Define the Metadata Model and Single Fetch Coroutine

First, add `httpx` to the project.

```
uv add httpx
```

The `pyproject.toml` dependencies section now includes `httpx`:

```
dependencies = [
    "httpx>=0.28",
]
```

Next, define the result type and the coroutine that fetches one URL.

```
import asyncio
from dataclasses import dataclass
from datetime import datetime, timezone

import httpx

@dataclass(frozen=True)
class MetadataResult:
    url: str
    title: str | None
    description: str | None
    status_code: int
    fetched_at: str

def _extract_title(html: str) -> str | None:
    start = html.lower().find("<title>")
    end = html.lower().find("</title>")
    if start == -1 or end == -1:
        return None
    return html[start + 7 : end].strip()

def _extract_description(html: str) -> str | None:
    name_attr = 'name="description"'
    idx = html.lower().find(name_attr)
    if idx == -1:
        return None
    content_idx = html.lower().find('content="', idx)
    if content_idx == -1:
        return None
    start = content_idx + 9
    end = html.find('"', start)
    if end == -1:
```

```
        return None
    return html[start:end].strip()

async def fetch_url_metadata(client: httpx.AsyncClient, url: str) ->
MetadataResult:
    response = await client.get(url)
    response.raise_for_status()
    text = response.text
    return MetadataResult(
        url=url,
        title=_extract_title(text),
        description=_extract_description(text),
        status_code=response.status_code,
        fetched_at=datetime.now(timezone.utc).isoformat(),
    )
```

`fetch_url_metadata` is a coroutine. It accepts a shared `httpx.AsyncClient` instance and a target URL. The helper functions perform minimal HTML parsing to extract the title and meta description without introducing heavy dependencies. `frozen=True` on the dataclass makes the result immutable and hashable.

`response.raise_for_status()` raises an `httpx.HTTPStatusError` whenever the server returns a non-2xx status code. We treat these as fetch failures rather than valid metadata. Non-2xx responses do not produce a `MetadataResult`; they raise.

Step 2: Execute a Single Coroutine from Synchronous Code

The tracker CLI is synchronous. `asyncio.run()` bridges the two worlds. The `async with` statement manages the `httpx.AsyncClient` lifecycle. It initializes the connection pool on entry and releases resources on exit. You'll use this pattern every time you create an async HTTP client.

```
def demo_single_fetch(url: str = "https://www.python.org") -> None:
    async def _inner() -> MetadataResult:
        async with httpx.AsyncClient() as client:
            return await fetch_url_metadata(client, url)

    result = asyncio.run(_inner())
    print(f"Fetched: {result.title} ({result.status_code})")
```

asyncio.run() handles event loop creation and teardown. It should be called once at the top-level entry point. Never call it inside an already running event loop.

Step 3: Fetch Multiple URLs Concurrently with TaskGroup

Fetching one URL at a time wastes wall-clock time when the network is the bottleneck. asyncio.TaskGroup spawns concurrent fetches and collects the results.

```
async def fetch_all_metadata(urls: list[str]) ->
list[MetadataResult]:
    async with httpx.AsyncClient() as client:
        async with asyncio.TaskGroup() as tg:
            tasks = [tg.create_task(fetch_url_metadata(client, u))
for u in urls]
    return [t.result() for t in tasks]
```

Each tg.create_task() schedules a coroutine on the event loop. The async with block waits until every task finishes. If one fetch raises an exception, the group cancels the others and propagates an ExceptionGroup. This prevents partial success states from leaking.

Step 4: Wire Async Fetching into a Tracker Command Handler

The tracker CLI remains synchronous. The new command handler loads notes through the guarded storage boundary, extracts valid source URLs, and delegates concurrent fetching to fetch_all_metadata. Because the fetches run inside asyncio.TaskGroup, any failed fetch (including an httpx network or status error) surfaces wrapped in an ExceptionGroup, so that is the handler that fires. The result is a clean failure message, matching the error-boundary style established in Chapter 9.

Synchronous callers need no changes.

```
import httpx

from knowledge_tracker.exceptions import StorageError
from knowledge_tracker.storage import NoteRepository,
load_notes_guarded

def run_fetch_metadata(repo: NoteRepository) -> str:
    try:
```

```
        notes = load_notes_guarded(repo)
    except StorageError as e:
        return f"Failed to load notes: {e}"

    urls = [n.source_url for n in notes if n.source_url and
n.has_source]
    if not urls:
        return "No notes with valid source URLs found."

    try:
        results = asyncio.run(fetch_all_metadata(urls))
    except ExceptionGroup as eg:
        first = eg.exceptions[0]
        return f"Batch fetch failed with {len(eg.exceptions)}
error(s); first: {first}"
    except Exception as e:
        return f"Unexpected fetch error: {e}"

    lines = [f"{r.status_code}  {r.url} -> {r.title}" for r in
results]
    return "\n".join(lines) if lines else "No metadata fetched."
```

The public function `run_fetch_metadata` remains synchronous so the existing `argparse` dispatcher needs no async refactoring. The async work is isolated behind `asyncio.run()`.

Step 5: Define a CPU-Bound Baseline

With the tracker's async I/O path established, the remainder of the chapter compares concurrency models for CPU-bound work. The following baseline function provides a measurable, CPU-intensive workload.

```
def cpu_bound_sum(n: int) -> int:
    total = 0
    for i in range(n):
        total += i * i
    return total
```

This function performs integer arithmetic in pure Python. Under the standard GIL build, only one thread executes this at a time.

Step 6: ThreadPoolExecutor under the Standard GIL

Threads are valid for concurrent I/O, but they do not parallelize CPU-bound Python code when the GIL is active.

```
import time
from concurrent.futures import ThreadPoolExecutor

def demo_thread_pool() -> None:
    numbers = [5_000_000] * 4
    start = time.perf_counter()
    with ThreadPoolExecutor(max_workers=4) as pool:
        list(pool.map(cpu_bound_sum, numbers))
    elapsed = time.perf_counter() - start
    print(f"ThreadPool (GIL): {elapsed:.2f}s")
```

On a standard `python3.14` interpreter, four workers complete this serially. Expect roughly four times the single-worker duration.

Step 7: Free-Threaded Python

Python 3.14 distributes a free-threaded binary called `python3.14t`. It disables the GIL, allowing threads to run Python bytecode in parallel.

```
import sys

def demo_free_threaded() -> None:
    numbers = [5_000_000] * 4
    start = time.perf_counter()
    with ThreadPoolExecutor(max_workers=4) as pool:
        list(pool.map(cpu_bound_sum, numbers))
    elapsed = time.perf_counter() - start
    print(f"ThreadPool (GIL={sys._is_gil_enabled()}):
{elapsed:.2f}s")
```

Run this script with the free-threaded interpreter to see significant speedup on multi-core machines. Install it with `uv python install 3.14t` and execute via `uv run --python 3.14t python ch10_async.py`. Under the standard build, the same code runs serially. `sys._is_gil_enabled()` returns `False` only under the free-threaded build.

Step 8: Multiprocessing for Process Isolation

Multiprocessing launches separate OS processes. Each process has its own Python interpreter and memory space. It avoids the GIL entirely, but serialization overhead is higher.

```
import multiprocessing
```

```
def demo_multiprocessing() -> None:
    numbers = [5_000_000] * 4
    start = time.perf_counter()
    with multiprocessing.Pool(processes=4) as pool:
        list(pool.map(cpu_bound_sum, numbers))
    elapsed = time.perf_counter() - start
    print(f"Multiprocessing: {elapsed:.2f}s")
```

On Windows and macOS, multiprocessing defaults to the `spawn` start method. Any code that invokes `multiprocessing.Pool` must run behind an `if __name__ == '__main__':` guard to prevent recursive process creation.

Omitting this guard causes cryptic crashes.

Use multiprocessing when CPU parallelism must be combined with strict memory isolation or when extension modules hold state that is not free-threaded safe.

Step 9: Subinterpreters for In-Process Isolation

Python 3.14 adds `concurrent.interpreters`. Each subinterpreter has its own GIL and module state. Communication happens through a queue.

The `create_queue()` call returns a `Queue` with `.put()` and `.get()` methods. The queue is shared into the worker's namespace through `prepare_main()`, allowing the subinterpreter to transmit data back to the host. The host reads with `.get()`.

```
def demo_subinterpreters() -> None:
    import concurrent.interpreters as interp

    queue = interp.create_queue()
    worker = interp.create()
    try:
        worker.prepare_main(queue=queue)
        worker.exec(
            "import sys\n"
            "queue.put(f'version {sys.version_info.minor}')"
        )
        print(f"Subinterpreter: {queue.get()}")
    finally:
        worker.close()
```

Subinterpreters suit plugin sandboxing or parallel CPU work where process spawn overhead is unacceptable. They are not a replacement for async I/O.

Full Example

The following module consolidates every new type and function introduced in this chapter. Place it at `src/knowledge_tracker/ch10_async.py`. It imports existing tracker types from the package and remains runnable as a script for demonstration.

```
# src/knowledge_tracker/ch10_async.py
import asyncio
import multiprocessing
import sys
import time
from concurrent.futures import ThreadPoolExecutor
from dataclasses import dataclass
from datetime import datetime, timezone

import httpx

from knowledge_tracker.exceptions import StorageError
from knowledge_tracker.storage import NoteRepository,
load_notes_guarded

@dataclass(frozen=True)
class MetadataResult:
    url: str
    title: str | None
    description: str | None
    status_code: int
    fetched_at: str

def _extract_title(html: str) -> str | None:
    start = html.lower().find("<title>")
    end = html.lower().find("</title>")
    if start == -1 or end == -1:
        return None
    return html[start + 7 : end].strip()

def _extract_description(html: str) -> str | None:
    name_attr = 'name="description"'
    idx = html.lower().find(name_attr)
    if idx == -1:
        return None
    content_idx = html.lower().find('content="', idx)
    if content_idx == -1:
        return None
    start = content_idx + 9
    end = html.find('"', start)
    if end == -1:
        return None
    return html[start:end].strip()

async def fetch_url_metadata(client: httpx.AsyncClient, url: str) ->
```

```
MetadataResult:
    response = await client.get(url)
    response.raise_for_status()
    text = response.text
    return MetadataResult(
        url=url,
        title=_extract_title(text),
        description=_extract_description(text),
        status_code=response.status_code,
        fetched_at=datetime.now(timezone.utc).isoformat(),
    )

def demo_single_fetch(url: str = "https://www.python.org") -> None:
    async def _inner() -> MetadataResult:
        async with httpx.AsyncClient() as client:
            return await fetch_url_metadata(client, url)

    result = asyncio.run(_inner())
    print(f"Fetched: {result.title} ({result.status_code})")

async def fetch_all_metadata(urls: list[str]) ->
list[MetadataResult]:
    async with httpx.AsyncClient() as client:
        async with asyncio.TaskGroup() as tg:
            tasks = [tg.create_task(fetch_url_metadata(client, u))
for u in urls]
    return [t.result() for t in tasks]

def run_fetch_metadata(repo: NoteRepository) -> str:
    try:
        notes = load_notes_guarded(repo)
    except StorageError as e:
        return f"Failed to load notes: {e}"

    urls = [n.source_url for n in notes if n.source_url and
n.has_source]
    if not urls:
        return "No notes with valid source URLs found."

    try:
        results = asyncio.run(fetch_all_metadata(urls))
    except ExceptionGroup as eg:
        first = eg.exceptions[0]
        return f"Batch fetch failed with {len(eg.exceptions)}
error(s); first: {first}"
    except Exception as e:
        return f"Unexpected fetch error: {e}"

    lines = [f"{r.status_code}  {r.url} -> {r.title}" for r in
results]
    return "\n".join(lines) if lines else "No metadata fetched."

def cpu_bound_sum(n: int) -> int:
    total = 0
```

```
    for i in range(n):
        total += i * i
    return total

def demo_thread_pool() -> None:
    numbers = [5_000_000] * 4
    start = time.perf_counter()
    with ThreadPoolExecutor(max_workers=4) as pool:
        list(pool.map(cpu_bound_sum, numbers))
    print(f"ThreadPool (GIL): {time.perf_counter() - start:.2f}s")

def demo_free_threaded() -> None:
    numbers = [5_000_000] * 4
    start = time.perf_counter()
    with ThreadPoolExecutor(max_workers=4) as pool:
        list(pool.map(cpu_bound_sum, numbers))
    print(f"ThreadPool (GIL={sys._is_gil_enabled()}):
{time.perf_counter() - start:.2f}s")

def demo_multiprocessing() -> None:
    numbers = [5_000_000] * 4
    start = time.perf_counter()
    with multiprocessing.Pool(processes=4) as pool:
        list(pool.map(cpu_bound_sum, numbers))
    print(f"Multiprocessing: {time.perf_counter() - start:.2f}s")

def demo_subinterpreters() -> None:
    import concurrent.interpreters as interp

    queue = interp.create_queue()
    worker = interp.create()
    try:
        worker.prepare_main(queue=queue)
        worker.exec(
            "import sys\n"
            "queue.put(f'version {sys.version_info.minor}')"
        )
        print(f"Subinterpreter: {queue.get()}")
    finally:
        worker.close()

if __name__ == "__main__":
    print("=== Single fetch ===")
    demo_single_fetch()
    print("\n=== Concurrency comparison ===")
    demo_thread_pool()
    demo_free_threaded()
    demo_multiprocessing()
    demo_subinterpreters()
```

The module separates I/O-bound async fetching from CPU-bound demonstrations. `run_fetch_metadata` plugs into the existing CLI dispatcher without requiring async rewrites upstream. The concurrency comparison functions stand alone. Run them under whichever interpreter invokes the script.

Common Mistakes

- **Calling a coroutine without `await` or `asyncio.run()`.** A coroutine object is returned, not the result. The caller silently gets `<coroutine object ...>` instead of data. Always bridge sync and async boundaries with `asyncio.run()`.
- **Using `asyncio.get_event_loop()` at application entry points.** Do not call `asyncio.get_event_loop()` to launch async work. Use `asyncio.run()` as the canonical entry point. Inside an already running coroutine, call `asyncio.get_running_loop()` if you need the current loop.
- **Ignoring `ExceptionGroup` from `asyncio.TaskGroup`.** When one task fails, TaskGroup cancels the rest and raises `ExceptionGroup`. Catch `ExceptionGroup` or inspect its `exceptions` attribute to handle partial failures.
- **Mixing blocking I/O inside async coroutines.** Calling synchronous HTTP libraries like `requests` inside a coroutine blocks the event loop and defeats concurrency. Use `httpx.AsyncClient` for network I/O inside async code.
- **Expecting thread-level CPU parallelism under the standard GIL build.** `ThreadPoolExecutor` does not speed up CPU-bound Python work when running `python3.14`. Use the free-threaded build, multiprocessing, or subinterpreters instead.
- **Creating a new `httpx.AsyncClient` per request.** Reuse one client across related requests in production code to benefit from connection pooling. Pass the client as an argument.
- **Using free-threaded Python for I/O-bound workloads.** The standard GIL build plus async I/O is simpler and incurs lower per-thread overhead. Reserve `python3.14t` for CPU-bound multithreading.

Performance and Production Considerations

Async I/O minimizes memory overhead for high-concurrency network work. A single thread can manage thousands of concurrent connections. Threads carry higher memory cost and context-switch overhead, so async is the right default for the tracker's metadata fetcher.

`asyncio.TaskGroup` prevents orphaned tasks and resource leaks. Use it instead of manual `asyncio.create_task` plus `asyncio.gather` in new code. The structured cancellation semantics match modern expectations for concurrent error handling.

Reuse `httpx.AsyncClient` across related requests. The client maintains an HTTP connection pool. Creating a new client per request eliminates that optimization and increases connection overhead. Pass the client into coroutines that need it.

I once profiled a scraper that exhausted the file descriptor table because it created a fresh `AsyncClient` for every request.

The standard CPython build serializes CPU-bound Python threads. Do not use `ThreadPoolExecutor` for CPU-intensive Python algorithms unless the process runs under `python3.14t`. Even then, free-threaded Python tends to run somewhat slower per thread than the GIL build, with the payoff coming from scaling work across multiple cores. Reserve `python3.14t` for CPU-bound multithreading.

Multiprocessing carries serialization and process spawn overhead. Avoid it for fine-grained tasks or high-frequency calls. It is the right choice when memory isolation between workers is mandatory.

Subinterpreters share process memory but isolate module state. They suit plugin systems or parallel CPU work where process overhead is too high. They do not replace async I/O for network concurrency.

Configure explicit timeouts on `httpx.AsyncClient` to prevent unresponsive hosts from hanging coroutines indefinitely. A project-specific configuration looks like this:

```
timeout = httpx.Timeout(10.0, connect=5.0)
async with httpx.AsyncClient(timeout=timeout) as client:
    ...
```

Log metadata fetch failures at the CLI boundary rather than printing raw tracebacks. The tracker already configures logging in Chapter 9. Wrap `httpx` exceptions and translate them into domain-level messages before returning to the user.

Summary

Async I/O with `async` and `await` is the modern Python approach to high-concurrency network operations. The Personal Knowledge Tracker CLI now enriches notes by fetching source URL metadata concurrently through `httpx.AsyncClient` and `asyncio.TaskGroup`. The synchronous CLI boundary remains intact; `asyncio.run()` executes the async subtree and returns results to the caller.

Python 3.14 expands the concurrency toolbox. The standard `python3.14` interpreter handles async I/O and threaded I/O concurrency. The opt-in `python3.14t` build removes the GIL and enables CPU-bound thread parallelism. Multiprocessing provides strict process isolation. Subinterpreters offer in-process isolation with lower overhead than full processes. Match the tool to the workload: async for I/O, free-threaded threads for CPU parallelism, multiprocessing for isolation, and subinterpreters for sandboxed execution inside a single process.

Key Terms

- **Coroutine**: A function declared with `async def` that can suspend execution at `await` points and resume later via the event loop.
- **`await`**: The keyword that yields control from a coroutine back to the event loop until the awaited operation completes.
- **Event loop**: The single-threaded scheduler that drives concurrent coroutine execution and switches between tasks when they await I/O.
- **`asyncio.TaskGroup`**: A context manager that runs multiple async tasks concurrently; if one task raises an exception, it cancels the remaining tasks and propagates an `ExceptionGroup`.
- **Structured concurrency**: A pattern where child tasks are bound to a parent scope; failure in one task triggers automatic cleanup of siblings.

- **Free-threaded Python**: The opt-in `python3.14t` interpreter build that disables the GIL, allowing true parallel execution of Python threads.
- **Global Interpreter Lock (GIL)**: A mutex in standard CPython that allows only one thread to execute Python bytecode at a time.
- **`concurrent.interpreters`**: The Python 3.14 standard library module for creating isolated subinterpreters inside a single process, each with its own GIL and module state.
- **`MetadataResult`**: The frozen dataclass in the Personal Knowledge Tracker CLI that stores fetched URL metadata, including title, description, status code, and timestamp.
- **Connection pooling**: Reusing an HTTP client instance across multiple requests to amortize TCP handshake overhead and improve throughput.

Mini Quiz

1. **A developer needs to reduce wall-clock time when fetching metadata for 50 note source URLs. Currently they use a synchronous loop with `requests.get`. Which change most directly reduces wall-clock time?**

   A. Replace `requests.get` with `httpx.get` inside the same synchronous loop

   B. Use `ThreadPoolExecutor` with 50 threads and keep `requests.get`

   C. Use `asyncio.TaskGroup` with `httpx.AsyncClient` to fetch URLs concurrently

   D. Switch to the `python3.14t` free-threaded interpreter

2. **Consider the following snippet inside a coroutine:**

```
async with httpx.AsyncClient() as client:
    response = await client.get(url)
    return response.text
```

Which statement about this code is true?

   A. The `async with` statement creates a new OS thread for each client.

   B. `client.get` blocks the event loop until the response arrives, preventing other coroutines from running.

   C. The `await` yields control back to the event loop so other tasks can run while waiting for the network.

   D. `httpx.AsyncClient` is only available in the free-threaded `python3.14t` build.

3. **Which function is the canonical entry point to run a top-level coroutine from synchronous code?**

   A. `asyncio.get_event_loop().run_until_complete()`

   B. `asyncio.run()`

   C. Calling the coroutine function directly, such as `main()`

   D. `threading.Thread(target=coroutine)`

4. **A team writes a pure-Python function that performs heavy mathematical transformations on large datasets. They want**

to use threads to utilize all CPU cores on a server. Which approach is correct?

A. Use the standard `python3.14` build with `ThreadPoolExecutor`

B. Use the `python3.14t` free-threaded build with `ThreadPoolExecutor`

C. Use the standard `python3.14` build with `asyncio.TaskGroup`

D. Use `concurrent.interpreters` and share mutable lists directly between workers

5. **In Python 3.14, which module provides isolated interpreter contexts that each possess their own GIL and communicate via channels?**

A. `multiprocessing`

B. `threading`

C. `concurrent.interpreters`

D. `asyncio`

Answers are provided in the Answer Key at the end of the book.

Activity

Add a `fetch` subcommand to the Personal Knowledge Tracker CLI that asynchronously fetches metadata for every note that has a source URL. Batch fetchers crash hard when one malformed URL raises an unhandled exception. The steps below prevent that exact failure mode.

- Add defensive error handling to `fetch_url_metadata` so that one unreachable URL does not crash the entire metadata batch. Wrap the `client.get` and `raise_for_status` calls in a `try/except httpx.HTTPError` block. On failure, return a degraded `MetadataResult` with `status_code` set to `0`, `title` set to `None`, and `description` set to a short error string such as `"Fetch failed: {error}"`. Because each fetch now handles its own error and returns a result, no task raises and `TaskGroup` never produces an `ExceptionGroup` for fetch failures, so `fetch_all_metadata` needs no changes.
- Register the new subcommand in `src/knowledge_tracker/cli.py`. Inside `build_enhanced_parser`, add:

```
  fetch_parser = subparsers.add_parser("fetch", help="Fetch metadata
for notes with source URLs")
  fetch_parser.set_defaults(command="fetch")
```

Inside `run_enhanced_cli`, add an `elif args.command == "fetch":` branch that calls `run_fetch_metadata(repo)` and prints the returned summary.

- Ensure `run_fetch_metadata` follows the Chapter 9 error-boundary pattern. With the degraded-result strategy above, fetch failures arrive as `MetadataResult` rows rather than exceptions, so the existing `except ExceptionGroup` and `except Exception` handlers stay as a defensive boundary for unexpected non-fetch errors and return a user-friendly message instead of letting any exception propagate to the user.
- Create two test notes using the tracker CLI: one with `--source-url https://www.python.org` and one with `--source-url https://invalid-domain-12345.example`.
- Run `uv run python -m knowledge_tracker fetch`. Verify that the output shows a successful title fetch for `python.org` and a failure entry for the invalid domain, without an unhandled exception.

- (Optional) Use `time.perf_counter()` to compare wall-clock time between fetching three URLs sequentially in a synchronous loop versus using `asyncio.TaskGroup` with `httpx.AsyncClient`. Record the speedup.

Chapter 11: Testing and Type Checking

What You Will Learn

- Organize tests under `tests/` mirroring `src/knowledge_tracker/`
- Write pytest functions using fixtures, parametrization, and temporary paths
- Verify domain exceptions and error translation with `pytest.raises`
- Test protocol-backed storage without relying on production file paths
- Mock async HTTP dependencies to test metadata extraction offline
- Run `uv run pytest`, `uv run mypy`, and `uv run ruff check .` as standard workflow commands

Prerequisites

- Completion of Chapter 8 (Classes, Dataclasses, and Protocols)
- Completion of Chapter 9 (Application Errors, Exceptions, and Logging)
- Completion of Chapter 10 (Async I/O and Concurrency Choices)
- Understanding of the source layout and package structure from Chapter 7

Concept Overview

Testing proves that the Personal Knowledge Tracker CLI behaves as intended. Without tests, every refactor is a gamble. pytest provides a lightweight framework where plain `assert` statements and automatic discovery replace the boilerplate of older tools. Fixtures inject isolated dependencies: an empty in-memory repository, a temporary JSON file. Tests never collide. Parametrization turns one function into an exhaustive validation suite.

A CI pipeline I worked on hit two-minute test suites because every test wrote to ephemeral JSON files instead of in-memory repositories. Fixtures that return fresh `InMemoryNoteRepository` instances dropped the runtime back under five seconds.

Static analysis catches mistakes that tests miss. mypy reads type hints across the `Note` dataclass, `NoteRepository` protocol, and command handlers to flag mismatches before execution. ruff performs fast linting to enforce style and catch bugs. Together, these tools form a safety net that lets you change the tracker with confidence.

Step-by-Step Implementation

This chapter assumes the project structure from Chapter 10 is in place. `src/knowledge_tracker/models.py` contains `Note`, `SearchQuery`, `make_note`, and `note_is_valid`, while `src/knowledge_tracker/storage.py` contains `InMemoryNoteRepository`, `JsonNoteRepository`, and `load_notes_guarded`. Domain exceptions live in `src/knowledge_tracker/exceptions.py`, validators in `src/knowledge_tracker/validators.py`, command handlers in `src/knowledge_tracker/commands.py`, and async metadata fetchers in `src/knowledge_tracker/ch10_async.py`.

Step 1: Configure the Project for Testing

Ruff was already added as a development dependency in Chapter 1. Add pytest and mypy:

```
uv add --dev pytest mypy
```

Update `pyproject.toml` with pytest and mypy configuration. The `[tool.pytest.ini_options]` section tells pytest where to discover tests. The `[tool.mypy]` section enforces strict checking against Python 3.14 syntax and targets the `src/` tree.

```
[tool.pytest.ini_options]
testpaths = ["tests"]

[tool.mypy]
python_version = "3.14"
files = ["src"]
warn_return_any = true
warn_unused_configs = true
disallow_untyped_defs = true
```

These declarations keep behavior consistent across local runs and CI. `uv run pytest` discovers tests under `tests/`, while `uv run mypy` analyzes the full `src/` tree for type correctness.

Step 2: Test Note Creation and Validation

Create `tests/test_models.py`. Start with basic assertions that verify `make_note` constructs a `Note` correctly and that `note_is_valid` rejects blank titles.

```
from knowledge_tracker.models import make_note, note_is_valid

def test_make_note_sets_fields() -> None:
    note = make_note("Python 3.14", "New features overview",
["python", "news"])
    assert note.title == "Python 3.14"
    assert note.body == "New features overview"
    assert note.tags == ["python", "news"]
    assert note.source_url is None
    assert note.id.startswith("note-python_3_14")
    assert note.created

def test_note_is_valid_rejects_blank_title() -> None:
    note = make_note("", "Some body", ["tag"])
    assert note_is_valid(note) is False
```

Each test is a plain function. pytest discovers it automatically because the name begins with `test_`. The assertions check concrete field values and boolean outcomes. No special assertion methods are required.

Step 3: Parametrize Validation Tests

Add a table-driven test that exercises many valid and invalid combinations in one function. This avoids copying and pasting nearly identical test bodies.

```
import pytest
from knowledge_tracker.models import make_note, note_is_valid

@pytest.mark.parametrize(
    ("title", "body", "expected"),
    [
        ("Valid Title", "Valid body", True),
        ("", "Valid body", False),
        ("Valid Title", "", False),
        ("   ", "Valid body", False),
        ("Valid Title", "   ", False),
    ],
```

```
)
def test_note_is_valid_variants(title: str, body: str, expected:
bool) -> None:
    note = make_note(title, body, ["tag"])
    assert note_is_valid(note) is expected
```

Parametrization expands into five independent test cases at runtime. If one combination fails, pytest reports the exact row that caused the failure.

Step 4: Test In-Memory Repository Behavior

Create `tests/test_storage.py`. Define a fixture that returns a fresh `InMemoryNoteRepository` for every test. pytest injects the fixture by matching the argument name.

```
import pytest
from knowledge_tracker.models import make_note, SearchQuery
from knowledge_tracker.storage import InMemoryNoteRepository

@pytest.fixture
def in_memory_repo() -> InMemoryNoteRepository:
    return InMemoryNoteRepository()

def test_repo_save_and_list(in_memory_repo: InMemoryNoteRepository) -
> None:
    note1 = make_note("First", "Body one", ["a"])
    note2 = make_note("Second", "Body two", ["b"])
    in_memory_repo.save(note1)
    in_memory_repo.save(note2)

    notes = in_memory_repo.list_all()
    assert len(notes) == 2
    assert notes[0].title == "First"
    assert notes[1].title == "Second"

def test_repo_search_by_text_and_tags(in_memory_repo:
InMemoryNoteRepository) -> None:
    in_memory_repo.save(make_note("Python tips", "Code better",
["python"]))
    in_memory_repo.save(make_note("Rust tips", "Systems code",
["rust"]))

    text_results = in_memory_repo.search(SearchQuery(text="python"))
    assert len(text_results) == 1
    assert text_results[0].title == "Python tips"

    tag_results = in_memory_repo.search(SearchQuery(tags=["rust"]))
    assert len(tag_results) == 1
    assert tag_results[0].title == "Rust tips"
```

Fixtures eliminate manual setup. Because `in_memory_repo` is recreated for each test, no state leaks between them. The tests verify the protocol contract without touching the filesystem.

Step 5: Test JSON Persistence with Temporary Paths

Use the built-in `tmp_path` fixture to give `JsonNoteRepository` a real file that is discarded after the test. This proves that save and load survive a process restart.

```
from pathlib import Path
import pytest
from knowledge_tracker.models import make_note, SearchQuery
from knowledge_tracker.storage import JsonNoteRepository

@pytest.fixture
def json_repo(tmp_path: Path) -> JsonNoteRepository:
    return JsonNoteRepository(path=tmp_path / "notes.json")

def test_json_repo_round_trip(json_repo: JsonNoteRepository) -> None:
    note = make_note("Persisted", "Save me", ["persist"])
    json_repo.save(note)

    fresh_repo = JsonNoteRepository(path=json_repo.path)
    notes = fresh_repo.list_all()
    assert len(notes) == 1
    assert notes[0].title == "Persisted"
    assert notes[0].tags == ["persist"]

def test_json_repo_search_survives_reload(json_repo:
JsonNoteRepository) -> None:
    json_repo.save(make_note("Searchable", "Find me", ["search"]))

    fresh_repo = JsonNoteRepository(path=json_repo.path)
    results = fresh_repo.search(SearchQuery(text="find"))
    assert len(results) == 1
    assert results[0].title == "Searchable"
```

`tmp_path` provides a `pathlib.Path` to a unique temporary directory managed by pytest. Constructing a fresh `JsonNoteRepository` with the same path reloads the JSON from disk, proving that data survives beyond the original instance. The test writes to it exactly as the production code writes to `~/.knowledge_tracker/notes.json`. pytest removes the directory automatically after the test completes.

Step 6: Verify Domain Exceptions and Error Translation

Create `tests/test_errors.py`. Use `pytest.raises` to assert that the correct exception type is raised and that guard functions include useful context.

```
from pathlib import Path
import pytest
from knowledge_tracker.models import make_note, Note
from knowledge_tracker.exceptions import NoteValidationError,
StorageError
from knowledge_tracker.validators import ensure_valid_note
from knowledge_tracker.storage import load_notes_guarded

def test_ensure_valid_note_raises() -> None:
    note = make_note("", "Missing title", ["tag"])
    with pytest.raises(NoteValidationError) as exc_info:
        ensure_valid_note(note)
    assert "title" in str(exc_info.value).lower()

def test_load_notes_guarded_translates_oserror() -> None:
    class BrokenRepo:
        path: Path | None = Path("/broken")

        def list_all(self) -> list[Note]:
            raise OSError("disk full")

    with pytest.raises(StorageError) as exc_info:
        load_notes_guarded(BrokenRepo())  # type: ignore[arg-type]
    assert "disk full" in str(exc_info.value)
    assert isinstance(exc_info.value.__cause__, OSError)
```

`pytest.raises` captures the exception so you can inspect its message. `BrokenRepo` is a minimal test double that forces a deterministic error path without touching the filesystem. The `# type: ignore[arg-type]` comment suppresses mypy's argument-type error. `BrokenRepo` does not formally implement the `NoteRepository` protocol, yet it satisfies the shape needed for this test. The second test confirms the translation. The original exception survives in `__cause__`.

Step 7: Build an Async HTTP Mock

Create `tests/test_async.py`. To test `fetch_url_metadata` without network access, construct an `httpx.AsyncClient` with a custom transport that returns canned HTML.

httpx separates the transport layer (the component that actually sends bytes over a wire) from the client. Replacing the transport lets you intercept every request and return a fully formed response without opening a socket.

```
import httpx

class _MockTransport(httpx.AsyncBaseTransport):
    def __init__(self, html: str, status_code: int = 200) -> None:
        self._html = html
        self._status_code = status_code

    async def handle_async_request(self, request: httpx.Request) ->
httpx.Response:
        return httpx.Response(self._status_code, text=self._html,
request=request)

def make_mock_client(html: str, status_code: int = 200) ->
httpx.AsyncClient:
    return httpx.AsyncClient(transport=_MockTransport(html,
status_code))
```

The transport implements `handle_async_request` and returns a fully formed `httpx.Response`. The client behaves like a real HTTP client, but every request resolves instantly with the provided text.

In one project, a test that called a live metadata API started failing every afternoon when the third-party rate limit reset; replacing the transport with `_MockTransport` eliminated the flakiness entirely.

Step 8: Test Async Metadata Fetching

Use the mock client to exercise `fetch_url_metadata`. To test `run_fetch_metadata` offline, patch `fetch_all_metadata` inside `knowledge_tracker.ch10_async`, the module where `run_fetch_metadata` looks it up. Patch the usage name, not the definition.

```
import asyncio
from unittest.mock import patch
from knowledge_tracker.ch10_async import fetch_url_metadata,
MetadataResult
from knowledge_tracker.ch10_async import run_fetch_metadata
from knowledge_tracker.models import make_note
from knowledge_tracker.storage import InMemoryNoteRepository

def test_fetch_url_metadata_extracts_fields() -> None:
    html = (
```

```
        "<html><head>"
        "<title>Test Page</title>"
        "<meta name=\"description\" content=\"A test\">"
        "</head></html>"
    )

    async def _inner() -> MetadataResult:
        async with make_mock_client(html) as client:
            return await fetch_url_metadata(client,
"https://example.com")

    result = asyncio.run(_inner())
    assert result.title == "Test Page"
    assert result.description == "A test"
    assert result.status_code == 200
    assert result.url == "https://example.com"

def test_run_fetch_metadata_returns_summary() -> None:
    repo = InMemoryNoteRepository()
    repo.save(make_note("Note 1", "Body", ["tag"],
source_url="https://a.com"))
    repo.save(make_note("Note 2", "Body", ["tag"]))

    fake = MetadataResult(
        url="https://a.com",
        title="Mock Title",
        description=None,
        status_code=200,
        fetched_at="2025-01-01T00:00:00",
    )

    async def _fake_fetch(urls: list[str]) -> list[MetadataResult]:
        return [fake]

    with patch("knowledge_tracker.ch10_async.fetch_all_metadata",
new=_fake_fetch):
        summary = run_fetch_metadata(repo)

    assert "200" in summary
    assert "Mock Title" in summary
    assert "https://a.com" in summary
```

`asyncio.run` drives the coroutine inside a synchronous test function. The mock client closes properly through `async with`. The second test replaces the network-bound `fetch_all_metadata` with a local coroutine that returns canned data. This keeps the test fast and deterministic. It still exercises the summary formatting logic.

Full Example

Below are the complete test files for the Personal Knowledge Tracker CLI. Copy them into `tests/` and run `uv run pytest`.

`tests/test_models.py`

```
import pytest
from knowledge_tracker.models import make_note, note_is_valid

def test_make_note_sets_fields() -> None:
    note = make_note("Python 3.14", "New features overview",
["python", "news"])
    assert note.title == "Python 3.14"
    assert note.body == "New features overview"
    assert note.tags == ["python", "news"]
    assert note.source_url is None
    assert note.id.startswith("note-python_3_14")
    assert note.created

def test_note_is_valid_rejects_blank_title() -> None:
    note = make_note("", "Some body", ["tag"])
    assert note_is_valid(note) is False

@pytest.mark.parametrize(
    ("title", "body", "expected"),
    [
        ("Valid Title", "Valid body", True),
        ("", "Valid body", False),
        ("Valid Title", "", False),
        ("   ", "Valid body", False),
        ("Valid Title", "   ", False),
    ],
)
def test_note_is_valid_variants(title: str, body: str, expected:
bool) -> None:
    note = make_note(title, body, ["tag"])
    assert note_is_valid(note) is expected
```

`tests/test_storage.py`

```
from pathlib import Path
import pytest
from knowledge_tracker.models import make_note, SearchQuery
from knowledge_tracker.storage import InMemoryNoteRepository,
JsonNoteRepository

@pytest.fixture
def in_memory_repo() -> InMemoryNoteRepository:
    return InMemoryNoteRepository()
```

```
def test_repo_save_and_list(in_memory_repo: InMemoryNoteRepository) -
> None:
    note1 = make_note("First", "Body one", ["a"])
    note2 = make_note("Second", "Body two", ["b"])
    in_memory_repo.save(note1)
    in_memory_repo.save(note2)
    notes = in_memory_repo.list_all()
    assert len(notes) == 2
    assert notes[0].title == "First"
    assert notes[1].title == "Second"

def test_repo_search_by_text_and_tags(in_memory_repo:
InMemoryNoteRepository) -> None:
    in_memory_repo.save(make_note("Python tips", "Code better",
["python"]))
    in_memory_repo.save(make_note("Rust tips", "Systems code",
["rust"]))
    text_results = in_memory_repo.search(SearchQuery(text="python"))
    assert len(text_results) == 1
    assert text_results[0].title == "Python tips"
    tag_results = in_memory_repo.search(SearchQuery(tags=["rust"]))
    assert len(tag_results) == 1
    assert tag_results[0].title == "Rust tips"

@pytest.fixture
def json_repo(tmp_path: Path) -> JsonNoteRepository:
    return JsonNoteRepository(path=tmp_path / "notes.json")

def test_json_repo_round_trip(json_repo: JsonNoteRepository) -> None:
    note = make_note("Persisted", "Save me", ["persist"])
    json_repo.save(note)
    fresh_repo = JsonNoteRepository(path=json_repo.path)
    notes = fresh_repo.list_all()
    assert len(notes) == 1
    assert notes[0].title == "Persisted"
    assert notes[0].tags == ["persist"]

def test_json_repo_search_survives_reload(json_repo:
JsonNoteRepository) -> None:
    json_repo.save(make_note("Searchable", "Find me", ["search"]))
    fresh_repo = JsonNoteRepository(path=json_repo.path)
    results = fresh_repo.search(SearchQuery(text="find"))
    assert len(results) == 1
    assert results[0].title == "Searchable"
```

tests/test_errors.py

```
from pathlib import Path
import pytest
from knowledge_tracker.models import make_note, Note
from knowledge_tracker.exceptions import NoteValidationError,
StorageError
```

```
from knowledge_tracker.validators import ensure_valid_note
from knowledge_tracker.storage import load_notes_guarded

def test_ensure_valid_note_raises() -> None:
    note = make_note("", "Missing title", ["tag"])
    with pytest.raises(NoteValidationError) as exc_info:
        ensure_valid_note(note)
    assert "title" in str(exc_info.value).lower()

def test_load_notes_guarded_translates_oserror() -> None:
    class BrokenRepo:
        path: Path | None = Path("/broken")

        def list_all(self) -> list[Note]:
            raise OSError("disk full")

    with pytest.raises(StorageError) as exc_info:
        load_notes_guarded(BrokenRepo())  # type: ignore[arg-type]
    assert "disk full" in str(exc_info.value)
    assert isinstance(exc_info.value.__cause__, OSError)
```

tests/test_async.py

```
import asyncio
from unittest.mock import patch
import httpx
from knowledge_tracker.ch10_async import fetch_url_metadata,
MetadataResult
from knowledge_tracker.ch10_async import run_fetch_metadata
from knowledge_tracker.models import make_note
from knowledge_tracker.storage import InMemoryNoteRepository

class _MockTransport(httpx.AsyncBaseTransport):
    def __init__(self, html: str, status_code: int = 200) -> None:
        self._html = html
        self._status_code = status_code

    async def handle_async_request(self, request: httpx.Request) ->
httpx.Response:
        return httpx.Response(self._status_code, text=self._html,
request=request)

def make_mock_client(html: str, status_code: int = 200) ->
httpx.AsyncClient:
    return httpx.AsyncClient(transport=_MockTransport(html,
status_code))

def test_fetch_url_metadata_extracts_fields() -> None:
    html = (
        "<html><head>"
        "<title>Test Page</title>"
        "<meta name=\"description\" content=\"A test\">"
```

```
        "</head></html>"
    )

    async def _inner() -> MetadataResult:
        async with make_mock_client(html) as client:
            return await fetch_url_metadata(client,
"https://example.com")

    result = asyncio.run(_inner())
    assert result.title == "Test Page"
    assert result.description == "A test"
    assert result.status_code == 200
    assert result.url == "https://example.com"

def test_run_fetch_metadata_returns_summary() -> None:
    repo = InMemoryNoteRepository()
    repo.save(make_note("Note 1", "Body", ["tag"],
source_url="https://a.com"))
    repo.save(make_note("Note 2", "Body", ["tag"]))
    fake = MetadataResult(
        url="https://a.com",
        title="Mock Title",
        description=None,
        status_code=200,
        fetched_at="2025-01-01T00:00:00",
    )
    async def _fake_fetch(urls: list[str]) -> list[MetadataResult]:
        return [fake]
    with patch("knowledge_tracker.ch10_async.fetch_all_metadata",
new=_fake_fetch):
        summary = run_fetch_metadata(repo)
    assert "200" in summary
    assert "Mock Title" in summary
    assert "https://a.com" in summary
```

Run the suite, type checker, and linter:

```
uv run pytest
uv run mypy
uv run ruff check .
```

The tests cover note construction, validation rules, in-memory and JSON repository contracts, exception translation, and async metadata extraction. The type checker validates protocol compliance across repository implementations. The linter catches style violations in seconds.

Common Mistakes

- **Using `assert` without `pytest.raises` for exception tests.** Writing `assert raises_my_error()` does not verify that the exception propagates. Use `with pytest.raises(MyError)` to prove the code path fails as intended.
- **Mutating a shared fixture instance.** A fixture that returns a mutable object must return a fresh instance on every test. Manual caching pollutes state across tests.
- **Testing against the production data directory.** Hard-coding `~/.knowledge_tracker/notes.json` in tests risks destroying real user data. Always use the `tmp_path` fixture for filesystem-bound tests.
- **Ignoring mypy errors inside test files.** Even tests benefit from type hints. Untyped test functions obscure mismatches between the setup and the assertion. Add `-> None` annotations and type the fixture arguments.
- **Calling async functions directly without an event loop.** Attempting to `await` a coroutine inside a synchronous test function raises `SyntaxError` or `RuntimeError`. Use `asyncio.run` for a single coroutine, or rely on `pytest-asyncio` for larger suites.
- **Relying on `ruff check` to find logic bugs.** Ruff enforces style and selected lint rules. It does not prove correctness. Always pair linting with pytest and mypy.

Performance and Production Considerations

Keep the test pyramid balanced. Unit tests for `note_is_valid` and `InMemoryNoteRepository` run in milliseconds. JSON repository tests exercise real I/O but remain fast because `tmp_path` uses local disk. Avoid hitting external URLs in CI; the mock transport keeps async tests offline and deterministic.

Type-checking the entire `src/` tree with mypy is slower than pytest for small projects. mypy caches results between runs, so incremental checks complete quickly. Pin `python_version = "3.14"` in `pyproject.toml` so mypy rejects syntax that is valid in newer releases but unavailable in the target interpreter.

Run the tools in sequence during pre-commit checks: `uv run ruff check .` first because it is nearly instantaneous, then `uv run mypy`, then `uv run pytest`. Failures at each stage prevent wasted time on deeper checks.

Do not test private implementation details. If a test imports `_make_note_id` or `_extract_title`, it couples the suite to internal structure that may change. Test through public functions such as `make_note` and `fetch_url_metadata`. This preserves your ability to refactor.

Summary

This chapter added a complete test suite to the Personal Knowledge Tracker CLI. You organized tests under `tests/` to mirror the source package, wrote plain assertions with pytest, and used fixtures to inject fresh repository instances. Parametrization compressed multiple validation scenarios into a single readable function. The `tmp_path` fixture isolated JSON persistence tests from the developer's machine. `pytest.raises` verified that domain exceptions fire when data is invalid and that low-level errors translate into `StorageError` with preserved causes.

You also mocked `httpx` at the transport layer to test metadata extraction without network access, and you patched `fetch_all_metadata` to exercise the command-level summary formatter offline. Finally, you integrated `mypy` for static type checking and `ruff check` for linting into the standard `uv run` workflow.

Tests and types do not slow development. They accelerate it by catching regressions immediately and documenting expected behavior in executable form. Maintain this suite as the tracker grows.

Key Terms

- **pytest fixture**: A function decorated with `@pytest.fixture` that pytest injects into test functions by name, providing isolated setup such as a fresh repository instance.
- **Parametrization**: The `@pytest.mark.parametrize` decorator that expands a single test function into multiple cases derived from a table of inputs.

- **pytest.raises**: A context manager that asserts a specific exception type is raised inside its block and exposes the captured exception for inspection.
- **tmp_path**: A built-in pytest fixture that supplies a unique temporary directory for the current test, automatically removed afterward.
- **Mock transport**: A custom implementation of `httpx.AsyncBaseTransport` that returns canned responses, allowing async HTTP tests to run without network access.
- **Patch target**: The import path passed to `unittest.mock.patch` that points to the namespace where a function is used, not where it is defined.
- **Regression**: A bug introduced by a code change; a test suite prevents regressions by failing when existing behavior breaks.

Mini Quiz

1. **Consider the following tests that share a fixture:**

```
@pytest.fixture
def repo():
    return InMemoryNoteRepository()

def test_save(repo):
    repo.save(make_note("A", "body", []))
    assert len(repo.list_all()) == 1

def test_empty(repo):
    assert len(repo.list_all()) == 0
```

What does the success of both tests prove about pytest fixtures?

A. Fixtures are executed once per module and shared across all tests

B. Fixtures return a fresh instance for every test function

C. `InMemoryNoteRepository` automatically resets its internal state between calls

D. pytest runs tests in parallel by default

2. **What is the primary purpose of `@pytest.mark.parametrize`?**

A. It automatically generates fixtures for each parameter value

B. It runs the same test logic against multiple inputs in a single function

C. It patches external network calls with mock data

D. It skips tests that do not match the current Python version

3. **Which test implementation correctly verifies that `ensure_valid_note` raises `NoteValidationError` when given a blank title?**

A. `assert ensure_valid_note(make_note("", "body", [])) is False`

B. `assert make_note("", "body", []).title == ""`

C. `with pytest.raises(NoteValidationError): ensure_valid_note(make_note("", "body", []))`

D. `try: ensure_valid_note(make_note("", "body", [])); assert False except: pass`

4. **A developer writes a synchronous test function containing the line `result = await fetch_url_metadata(client, url)`. What happens when pytest collects this file?**

   A. The test passes because pytest automatically creates an event loop

   B. A `SyntaxError` occurs because `await` is invalid outside an async function

   C. The coroutine object is returned but never awaited, causing the assertion to fail

   D. pytest skips the test because it lacks the `@pytest.mark.asyncio` decorator

5. **When using `unittest.mock.patch` to replace `fetch_all_metadata` where it is looked up inside `knowledge_tracker.ch10_async`, which target string is correct?**

   A. `knowledge_tracker.ch10_async.fetch_all_metadata`

   B. `knowledge_tracker.commands.fetch_all_metadata`

   C. `fetch_all_metadata`

   D. `unittest.mock.fetch_all_metadata`

6. **What does the built-in `tmp_path` fixture provide during a test such as `test_json_repo_round_trip`?**

   A. A permanent directory inside the user's home folder

   B. A unique temporary directory that is cleaned up after the test

   C. A patched `pathlib.Path` that prevents all filesystem access

   D. Random JSON data for property-based testing

Answers are provided in the Answer Key at the end of the book.

Activity

- Create a new test file at `tests/test_commands.py` to exercise the command handlers introduced in Chapter 9.
- Import `argparse`, `pytest`, `InMemoryNoteRepository`, `run_create_logged`, `run_list_logged`, and `NoteValidationError`.
- Define a pytest fixture named `repo` that returns a fresh `InMemoryNoteRepository` instance for every test.
- Write `test_create_logged_success` that constructs `args = argparse.Namespace(title="CLI Test", body="Testing commands", tag=["pytest"], source_url=None)`, calls `run_create_logged(repo, args)`, and asserts the returned string contains "Created".
- Write `test_create_logged_rejects_blank_title` that constructs `args = argparse.Namespace(title="   ", body="Body", tag=[], source_url=None)` and verifies `run_create_logged` raises `NoteValidationError` using `pytest.raises`.
- Write `test_list_logged_enforces_positive_limit` that constructs `args = argparse.Namespace(limit=-1)` and verifies `run_list_logged` raises `NoteValidationError`.
- Run the new tests with `uv run pytest tests/test_commands.py -v`.
- Run the type checker against the new file with `uv run mypy tests/test_commands.py` and add any missing annotations needed to clear mypy warnings.

Chapter 12: Toolchain, Configuration, Performance, and Deployment

What You Will Learn

- Generate and commit a `uv.lock` file to guarantee identical dependency trees across machines
- Configure Ruff, mypy, and pytest in a single `pyproject.toml`
- Load typed application configuration from environment variables and override it with CLI flags
- Profile a slow operation with `cProfile` and interpret the resulting statistics
- Register a console script entry point so the tracker runs as `knowledge-tracker`
- Execute the project in CI and build a container image ready for production deployment

Prerequisites

- Completion of Chapter 7 (Modules, Packages, and Project Layout) for source layout, `pyproject.toml` metadata, and package imports
- Completion of Chapter 8 (Classes, Dataclasses, and Protocols) for the `Note` dataclass, `JsonNoteRepository`, `NoteRepository` protocol, and `SearchQuery`
- Completion of Chapter 9 (Application Errors, Exceptions, and Logging) for the custom exception hierarchy, `configure_logging`, guarded storage functions, and `run_resilient_cli` patterns
- Completion of Chapter 11 (Testing and Type Checking) for `pytest` discovery, fixtures, and basic `ruff` / `mypy` invocation

Concept Overview

Shipping the Personal Knowledge Tracker CLI requires more than correct code. A production-ready tool must install the same dependencies on every machine, expose its version, respect runtime settings from the environment, and profile cleanly in a container. Closing the loop that began in Chapter 1 with `uv init`, you will lock the dependency graph, centralize tool configuration, wire environment variables into a typed `TrackerConfig`, add global CLI flags, expose a console script entry point, and wrap the export workflow in `cProfile`. The final result is a repeatable, observable, and deployable Python 3.14 application.

Step-by-Step Implementation

Step 1: Reproducible Environments

A `pyproject.toml` declares intent. The `uv.lock` file records reality, pinning exact versions and cryptographic hashes for every transitive dependency. After adding or upgrading a package, regenerate the lockfile and commit it.

```
uv add httpx
uv add --dev pytest ruff mypy
uv sync
git add uv.lock pyproject.toml
git commit -m "Add httpx and lock dependencies"
```

Running `uv sync` on another machine (or in CI) recreates the exact environment from the lockfile. No drift. No surprise upgrades.

I once traced a CI failure to an uncommitted `uv.lock` and a patch release of `httpx` that landed between the developer's last sync and the CI runner's first.

Commit the lockfile. A project without a committed lockfile isn't reproducible.

Step 2: Unified Tool Configuration

Modern Python tooling converges on `pyproject.toml` as the single source of truth. Ruff, mypy, and pytest all read from this file, so configuration lives next to the project metadata it describes.

```
[project]
```

```
name = "knowledge-tracker"
version = "0.1.0"
description = "Personal Knowledge Tracker CLI"
requires-python = ">=3.14"
dependencies = [
    "httpx>=0.28",
]

[dependency-groups]
dev = [
    "pytest>=8.3",
    "ruff>=0.8",
    "mypy>=1.14",
]

[tool.ruff]
line-length = 100
target-version = "py314"

[tool.ruff.lint]
select = ["E", "F", "I", "B", "UP", "SIM"]

[tool.mypy]
python_version = "3.14"
strict = true
warn_return_any = true
warn_unused_ignores = true

[tool.pytest.ini_options]
testpaths = ["tests"]
```

Ruff's `target-version = "py314"` tells Ruff to assume Python 3.14 as the target, so its upgrade and compatibility rules behave correctly for that version and it won't suggest rewrites that only work on older or newer interpreters. mypy's `strict = true` catches missing return annotations and untyped function bodies. pytest discovers tests under `tests/` automatically.

Step 3: Typed Environment Configuration

Environment variables are the standard interface for runtime configuration. The `TrackerConfig` dataclass loads them with typed defaults, converting strings to the correct Python types immediately. It uses `Path` for filesystem locations so that directory operations remain cross-platform and explicit.

```
import os
from dataclasses import dataclass
from pathlib import Path
import importlib.metadata
```

```python
from knowledge_tracker.exceptions import TrackerError

@dataclass(frozen=True)
class TrackerConfig:
    data_dir: Path
    log_level: str
    default_limit: int

def load_config_from_env() -> TrackerConfig:
    raw_limit = os.getenv("KNOWLEDGE_TRACKER_DEFAULT_LIMIT", "20")
    try:
        default_limit = int(raw_limit)
    except ValueError as exc:
        raise TrackerError(
            f"Invalid KNOWLEDGE_TRACKER_DEFAULT_LIMIT: {raw_limit!r}"
        ) from exc

    raw_dir = os.getenv(
        "KNOWLEDGE_TRACKER_DATA_DIR",
        "~/.knowledge_tracker",
    )

    return TrackerConfig(
        data_dir=Path(raw_dir).expanduser(),
        log_level=os.getenv("KNOWLEDGE_TRACKER_LOG_LEVEL", "INFO"),
        default_limit=default_limit,
    )

def get_tracker_version() -> str:
    try:
        return importlib.metadata.version("knowledge-tracker")
    except importlib.metadata.PackageNotFoundError:
        return "unknown"
```

`frozen=True` makes the config immutable after creation. `Path.expanduser` resolves ~ correctly on both Unix and Windows. Invalid integer values for the limit raise `TrackerError` with a clear message rather than a raw `ValueError`. `importlib.metadata.version` reads the version declared in `[project]` of `pyproject.toml`, so the application always reports the installed package version rather than a hard-coded string. If the package isn't installed, it returns `"unknown"`.

Step 4: Production CLI Entry Point

Global flags for `--data-dir`, `--log-level`, and `--version` belong on the main parser, not inside subcommands, because they affect the entire CLI session regardless of which subcommand runs. argparse parses main-parser flags before dispatching to the subcommand handler. The entry point resolves configuration in priority order: CLI flags override environment variables, which override coded defaults.

```
import argparse
import logging
import sys
from pathlib import Path

from knowledge_tracker.commands import (
    run_create_logged,
    run_export_logged,
    run_list_logged,
    run_search_logged,
)
from knowledge_tracker.config import load_config_from_env,
get_tracker_version
from knowledge_tracker.exceptions import TrackerError, StorageError
from knowledge_tracker.logging_config import configure_logging
from knowledge_tracker.storage import JsonNoteRepository

def build_final_parser() -> argparse.ArgumentParser:
    parser = argparse.ArgumentParser(prog="knowledge-tracker")
    parser.add_argument("--data-dir", default=None, help="Override
data directory")
    parser.add_argument("--log-level", default=None, help="Override
log level")
    parser.add_argument(
        "--version",
        action="version",
        version=get_tracker_version(),
    )

    subparsers = parser.add_subparsers(dest="command", required=True)

    create = subparsers.add_parser("create")
    create.add_argument("title")
    create.add_argument("body")
    create.add_argument("--tag", action="append", default=[])

    list_ = subparsers.add_parser("list")
    list_.add_argument("--limit", type=int, default=None)

    search = subparsers.add_parser("search")
    search.add_argument("query", nargs="?", default="")
    search.add_argument("--tag", action="append", default=[])
    search.add_argument("--limit", type=int, default=None)

    export = subparsers.add_parser("export")
    export.add_argument("--output", default=None)

    return parser
```

```
def run_final_cli() -> None:
    config = load_config_from_env()
    args = build_final_parser().parse_args()

    data_dir = Path(args.data_dir).expanduser() if args.data_dir else
config.data_dir
    log_level_str = (args.log_level or config.log_level).upper()

    valid_levels = {"DEBUG", "INFO", "WARNING", "ERROR", "CRITICAL"}
    if log_level_str not in valid_levels:
        print(
            f"Invalid log level: {log_level_str}. "
            f"Use one of: {', '.join(sorted(valid_levels))}",
            file=sys.stderr,
        )
        sys.exit(1)

    level = getattr(logging, log_level_str)
    configure_logging(level=level)

    try:
        repo = JsonNoteRepository(data_dir / "notes.json")
    except OSError as exc:
        raise StorageError(
            f"Failed to initialize storage at {data_dir}"
        ) from exc

    try:
        if args.command == "create":
            result = run_create_logged(repo, args)
        elif args.command == "list":
            if args.limit is None:
                args.limit = config.default_limit
            result = run_list_logged(repo, args)
        elif args.command == "search":
            result = run_search_logged(repo, args)
        elif args.command == "export":
            result = run_export_logged(repo, args)
        else:
            result = "Unknown command"
        print(result)
    except TrackerError as exc:
        logging.getLogger("knowledge_tracker.cli").exception("Command
failed")
        print(f"Error: {exc}", file=sys.stderr)
        sys.exit(1)
```

`run_final_cli` validates the log level before initializing the logging system, expands user paths for both environment and CLI overrides, initializes the repository once, and translates initialization failures into `StorageError`. The default limit applies only when the user omits `--limit`. Domain errors route to stderr while full tracebacks go to the log, preserving the boundary pattern from Chapter 9. This composition adds typed configuration to the same resilient boundary.

Step 5: Performance Profiling

When the Zstandard export slows down on large note collections, you need data, not guesses. `cProfile` measures call frequency and cumulative time. Wrap the export operation, then sort statistics by cumulative time to find the bottleneck.

```
import cProfile
import pstats
from pathlib import Path

from knowledge_tracker.export import export_archive_guarded
from knowledge_tracker.storage import JsonNoteRepository

def profile_export_operation(notes_path: Path, archive_path: Path) ->
None:
    repo = JsonNoteRepository(notes_path)
    notes = repo.list_all()

    profiler = cProfile.Profile()
    profiler.enable()
    try:
        export_archive_guarded(notes, archive_path)
    finally:
        profiler.disable()

    stats = pstats.Stats(profiler)
    stats.sort_stats(pstats.SortKey.CUMULATIVE)
    stats.print_stats(10)
```

Run the profiler offline against your real data file:

```
uv run python -c "
from pathlib import Path
from knowledge_tracker.profiler import profile_export_operation
profile_export_operation(
    Path.home() / '.knowledge_tracker' / 'notes.json',
    Path('notes.json.zst'),
)
"
```

Sample output:

```
        4203 function calls (4181 primitive calls) in 0.015 seconds

   Ordered by: cumulative time
   List reduced from 45 to 10 due to restriction <10>

   ncalls  tottime  percall  cumtime  percall
filename:lineno(function)
        1    0.000    0.000    0.015    0.015 {built-in method
builtins.exec}
        1    0.000    0.000    0.015    0.015 <string>:1(<module>)
        1    0.000    0.000    0.015    0.015
profiler.py:12(profile_export_operation)
        1    0.000    0.000    0.012    0.012
export.py:45(export_archive_guarded)
        1    0.010    0.010    0.010    0.010
export.py:58(compress_payload)
       12    0.001    0.000    0.002    0.000 json.py:183(dump)
     ...
```

The `cumtime` column shows the total time spent in a function and all its callees. `tottime` shows only the function body time. When `cumtime` is high but `tottime` is low, the bottleneck lives in callees. In this sample, `compress_payload` dominates `tottime`. The compression step is the expensive operation.

Don't profile in production. Profiling belongs in offline benchmarks.

Step 6: Packaging and Entry Points

A console script entry point installs the CLI into the virtual environment's `bin` directory. After `uv sync`, the tracker runs as `knowledge-tracker` from any working directory.

```
[project.scripts]
knowledge-tracker = "knowledge_tracker.cli:run_final_cli"
```

The `__main__.py` module remains useful for `python -m knowledge_tracker`, but the console script is the primary user-facing interface. If you created `__main__.py` back in Chapter 7, update its import to the final entry point name: `from knowledge_tracker.cli import run_final_cli` (the CLI entry function was renamed as the app evolved across chapters). The final CLI exposes the `create`, `list`, `search`, and `export` commands; the asynchronous metadata fetch from Chapter 10 is intentionally left as a future extension and is not registered as a subcommand.

Step 7: CI and Container Execution

Continuous integration (CI) is the practice of automatically building and testing code on every push or pull request. A minimal GitHub Actions workflow installs uv, selects Python 3.14, syncs from the lockfile, and runs the standard commands.

```
name: CI

on:
  push:
    branches: [main]
  pull_request:
    branches: [main]

jobs:
  test:
    runs-on: ubuntu-latest
    steps:
      - uses: actions/checkout@v4

      - name: Install uv
        uses: astral-sh/setup-uv@v5

      - name: Install Python 3.14
        run: uv python install 3.14

      - name: Sync dependencies
        run: uv sync --frozen

      - name: Run tests
        run: uv run pytest

      - name: Type check
        run: uv run mypy src

      - name: Lint
        run: uv run ruff check .

      - name: Check formatting
        run: uv run ruff format --check .
```

`setup-uv` adds uv to `PATH` automatically. `uv python install 3.14` ensures the exact interpreter is available, and `uv sync --frozen` recreates the environment from the committed lockfile without upgrading.

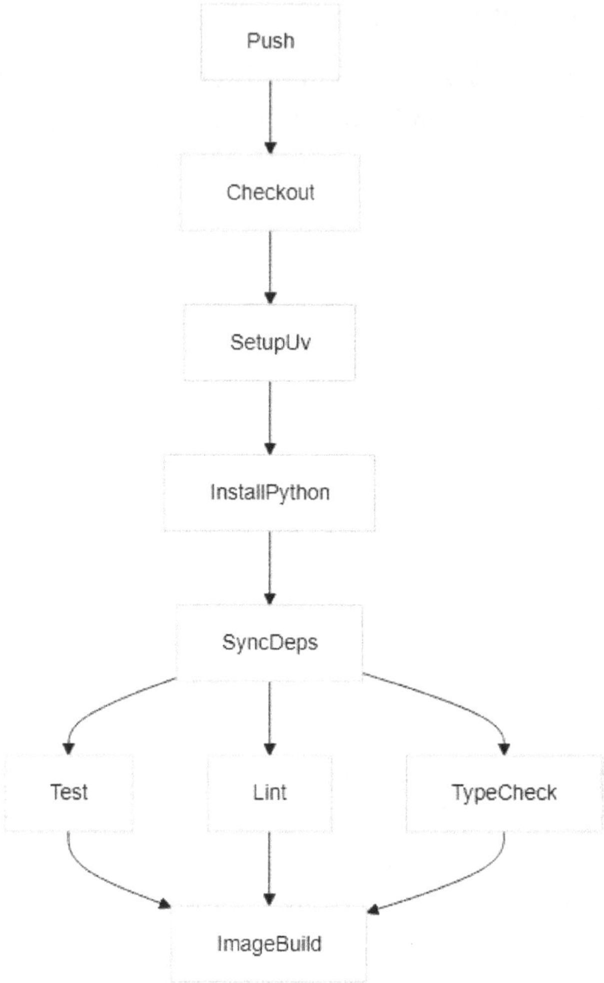

For deployment, a slim container image copies the lockfile and source, then installs production dependencies only.

```
FROM python:3.14-slim

COPY --from=ghcr.io/astral-sh/uv:latest /uv /usr/local/bin/uv

WORKDIR /app
COPY pyproject.toml uv.lock .python-version ./
COPY src ./src

RUN uv sync --frozen --no-dev

ENV KNOWLEDGE_TRACKER_DATA_DIR=/data
VOLUME ["/data"]

ENTRYPOINT ["uv", "run", "--no-dev", "knowledge-tracker"]
```

The `COPY --from=ghcr.io/astral-sh/uv:latest` instruction copies the standalone uv binary from the official Astral container image into the final Python image. This avoids installing curl or package managers in the production layer. The `--frozen` flag prevents uv from attempting to update the lockfile during the build. The `--no-dev` flag excludes pytest and mypy from the image, keeping the final layer small.

Full Example

The following files consolidate the chapter's production configuration and entry points.

```
# pyproject.toml (selected sections)
[project]
name = "knowledge-tracker"
version = "0.1.0"
description = "Personal Knowledge Tracker CLI"
requires-python = ">=3.14"
dependencies = [
    "httpx>=0.28",
]

[dependency-groups]
dev = [
    "pytest>=8.3",
    "ruff>=0.8",
    "mypy>=1.14",
]

[project.scripts]
knowledge-tracker = "knowledge_tracker.cli:run_final_cli"

[tool.ruff]
line-length = 100
target-version = "py314"

[tool.ruff.lint]
select = ["E", "F", "I", "B", "UP", "SIM"]

[tool.mypy]
python_version = "3.14"
strict = true
warn_return_any = true
warn_unused_ignores = true

[tool.pytest.ini_options]
testpaths = ["tests"]
```

```python
# src/knowledge_tracker/config.py
import os
from dataclasses import dataclass
from pathlib import Path
import importlib.metadata

from knowledge_tracker.exceptions import TrackerError

@dataclass(frozen=True)
class TrackerConfig:
    data_dir: Path
    log_level: str
    default_limit: int

def load_config_from_env() -> TrackerConfig:
    raw_limit = os.getenv("KNOWLEDGE_TRACKER_DEFAULT_LIMIT", "20")
    try:
        default_limit = int(raw_limit)
    except ValueError as exc:
        raise TrackerError(
            f"Invalid KNOWLEDGE_TRACKER_DEFAULT_LIMIT: {raw_limit!r}"
        ) from exc

    raw_dir = os.getenv(
        "KNOWLEDGE_TRACKER_DATA_DIR",
        "~/.knowledge_tracker",
    )

    return TrackerConfig(
        data_dir=Path(raw_dir).expanduser(),
        log_level=os.getenv("KNOWLEDGE_TRACKER_LOG_LEVEL", "INFO"),
        default_limit=default_limit,
    )

def get_tracker_version() -> str:
    try:
        return importlib.metadata.version("knowledge-tracker")
    except importlib.metadata.PackageNotFoundError:
        return "unknown"
```

```python
# src/knowledge_tracker/cli.py
import argparse
import logging
import sys
from pathlib import Path

from knowledge_tracker.commands import (
    run_create_logged,
    run_export_logged,
    run_list_logged,
    run_search_logged,
```

```
)
from knowledge_tracker.config import load_config_from_env,
get_tracker_version
from knowledge_tracker.exceptions import TrackerError, StorageError
from knowledge_tracker.logging_config import configure_logging
from knowledge_tracker.storage import JsonNoteRepository

def build_final_parser() -> argparse.ArgumentParser:
    parser = argparse.ArgumentParser(prog="knowledge-tracker")
    parser.add_argument("--data-dir", default=None, help="Override
data directory")
    parser.add_argument("--log-level", default=None, help="Override
log level")
    parser.add_argument(
        "--version",
        action="version",
        version=get_tracker_version(),
    )

    subparsers = parser.add_subparsers(dest="command", required=True)

    create = subparsers.add_parser("create")
    create.add_argument("title")
    create.add_argument("body")
    create.add_argument("--tag", action="append", default=[])

    list_ = subparsers.add_parser("list")
    list_.add_argument("--limit", type=int, default=None)

    search = subparsers.add_parser("search")
    search.add_argument("query", nargs="?", default="")
    search.add_argument("--tag", action="append", default=[])
    search.add_argument("--limit", type=int, default=None)

    export = subparsers.add_parser("export")
    export.add_argument("--output", default=None)

    return parser

def run_final_cli() -> None:
    config = load_config_from_env()
    args = build_final_parser().parse_args()

    data_dir = Path(args.data_dir).expanduser() if args.data_dir else
config.data_dir
    log_level_str = (args.log_level or config.log_level).upper()

    valid_levels = {"DEBUG", "INFO", "WARNING", "ERROR", "CRITICAL"}
    if log_level_str not in valid_levels:
        print(
            f"Invalid log level: {log_level_str}. "
            f"Use one of: {', '.join(sorted(valid_levels))}",
            file=sys.stderr,
        )
```

```
        sys.exit(1)

    level = getattr(logging, log_level_str)
    configure_logging(level=level)

    try:
        repo = JsonNoteRepository(data_dir / "notes.json")
    except OSError as exc:
        raise StorageError(
            f"Failed to initialize storage at {data_dir}"
        ) from exc

    try:
        if args.command == "create":
            result = run_create_logged(repo, args)
        elif args.command == "list":
            if args.limit is None:
                args.limit = config.default_limit
            result = run_list_logged(repo, args)
        elif args.command == "search":
            result = run_search_logged(repo, args)
        elif args.command == "export":
            result = run_export_logged(repo, args)
        else:
            result = "Unknown command"
        print(result)
    except TrackerError as exc:
        logging.getLogger("knowledge_tracker.cli").exception("Command
failed")
        print(f"Error: {exc}", file=sys.stderr)
        sys.exit(1)
```

```
# src/knowledge_tracker/profiler.py
import cProfile
import pstats
from pathlib import Path

from knowledge_tracker.export import export_archive_guarded
from knowledge_tracker.storage import JsonNoteRepository

def profile_export_operation(notes_path: Path, archive_path: Path) ->
None:
    repo = JsonNoteRepository(notes_path)
    notes = repo.list_all()

    profiler = cProfile.Profile()
    profiler.enable()
    try:
        export_archive_guarded(notes, archive_path)
    finally:
        profiler.disable()
```

```
    stats = pstats.Stats(profiler)
    stats.sort_stats(pstats.SortKey.CUMULATIVE)
    stats.print_stats(10)
```

```
# Dockerfile
FROM python:3.14-slim

COPY --from=ghcr.io/astral-sh/uv:latest /uv /usr/local/bin/uv

WORKDIR /app
COPY pyproject.toml uv.lock .python-version ./
COPY src ./src

RUN uv sync --frozen --no-dev

ENV KNOWLEDGE_TRACKER_DATA_DIR=/data
VOLUME ["/data"]

ENTRYPOINT ["uv", "run", "--no-dev", "knowledge-tracker"]
```

The `config` module isolates environment parsing from CLI logic. The `cli` module composes configuration, logging, and dispatch. The `profiler` module provides an offline benchmark harness for the export path. Together, these files turn the Personal Knowledge Tracker from a development script into an installable, observable, and deployable tool.

Common Mistakes

- **Ignoring the lockfile in version control.** `uv.lock` guarantees identical dependencies. Without it, CI and teammates resolve floating versions. Add `uv.lock` to git and treat it as source code.
- **Storing secrets in `pyproject.toml`.** TOML is committed to version control. Database passwords and API keys belong in environment variables, not tool configuration.
- **Forgetting type conversion on environment variables.** `os.environ` stores strings. Passing a non-numeric string like `"twenty"` to `int()` raises `ValueError`. Dataclass annotations do not perform runtime validation; you must convert and validate explicitly before construction.

- **Profiling in production.** `cProfile` adds significant overhead. Run benchmarks offline against representative data. Production commands stay unprofiled.
- **Using the wrong distribution name with `importlib.metadata`.** The name passed to `version()` must match `[project].name` in `pyproject.toml` exactly. Mismatches raise `PackageNotFoundError`.

Performance and Production Considerations

- `uv sync` with a committed lockfile resolves dependencies in milliseconds. Re-sync after every `pyproject.toml` change to keep the lockfile current.
- `TrackerConfig` loads once at process startup. Avoid repeated `os.getenv` calls inside hot loops; the environment does not change during a single CLI invocation.
- The standard `python3.14` binary outperforms `python3.14t` for single-threaded workloads. Use the default GIL build for CLI tools. Free-threading is for CPU-bound parallel work (Chapter 10).
- Container builds use `uv sync --frozen --no-dev`. The `--frozen` flag prevents lockfile updates, and `--no-dev` excludes test frameworks and type checkers from the image.
- `cProfile` output is verbose. Pipe `pstats` to a file for offline analysis: `stats.dump_stats("export.prof")`. Visualize bottlenecks with `snakeviz` for deeper inspection.

Summary

You have finalized the Personal Knowledge Tracker CLI as a reproducible Python 3.14 application. You committed `uv.lock` to eliminate dependency drift, centralized Ruff, mypy, and pytest configuration in `pyproject.toml`, and loaded typed runtime settings from the environment via `TrackerConfig`. The production entry point added global flags for `--data-dir` and `--log-level`, validated inputs before use, exposed a console script, and preserved the error boundaries from Chapter 9. Offline profiling with `cProfile` gave you a concrete way to measure export performance, while the Dockerfile and GitHub Actions workflow provided a template for automated testing and container deployment. The tracker is now ready for local development, CI validation, and production execution.

Key Terms

- **uv.lock**: It's a machine-generated lockfile that records exact dependency versions and cryptographic hashes. Commit it to version control for reproducible environments.
- **Console script entry point**: A `[project.scripts]` declaration in `pyproject.toml` that installs a callable into the virtual environment's bin directory.
- **importlib.metadata**: The standard-library module for reading package metadata, such as version strings, from the installed environment.
- **TrackerConfig**: An immutable dataclass that loads runtime settings from environment variables and CLI flags, resolving filesystem paths as `pathlib.Path` objects with typed defaults.
- **cProfile**: The standard-library profiler that measures function call frequency and execution time for offline bottleneck analysis.
- **--frozen**: A `uv sync` flag that prevents the lockfile from being updated during installation; use it in CI and container builds.
- **--no-dev**: A `uv sync` flag that excludes development dependencies, such as pytest and mypy, from the installed environment.

Mini Quiz

1. **Why should `uv.lock` be committed to version control?**

   A. It replaces the need for `pyproject.toml`

   B. It pins exact dependency versions and hashes for reproducible builds

   C. It stores sensitive credentials for CI authentication

   D. It declares the minimum Python version for the project

2. **When resolving the data directory for the tracker, which source takes precedence?**

   A. The hard-coded default in `TrackerConfig`

   B. The `KNOWLEDGE_TRACKER_DATA_DIR` environment variable

   C. The `--data-dir` CLI flag passed at runtime

   D. The `.python-version` file in the project root

3. **Which standard-library function retrieves the application version from the installed package metadata?**

   A. `os.getenv`

   B. `importlib.metadata.version`

   C. `argparse.ArgumentParser.parse_args`

   D. `logging.getLogger`

4. **What is the correct context for running `cProfile` against the export operation?**

   A. Inside the production Docker entrypoint on every export

   B. During every CI test run as a mandatory check

   C. In an offline benchmark with representative data

   D. Inside the `run_final_cli` function during normal usage

5. **In the production Dockerfile, what does the `uv sync --frozen --no-dev` command accomplish?**

   A. It updates the lockfile to the latest PyPI releases

   B. It prevents lockfile changes and excludes development dependencies

   C. It installs only packages listed in `requirements.txt`

   D. It enables the free-threaded Python interpreter

Answers are provided in the Answer Key at the end of the book.

Activity

- Open `src/knowledge_tracker/cli.py` and add a new `config` subcommand to `build_final_parser`. The subcommand needs no arguments of its own.
- In `run_final_cli`, add a branch for `args.command == "config"`. Inside that branch, load the configuration with `load_config_from_env()`, apply any CLI overrides, call `get_tracker_version()`, and print the fully resolved config fields alongside the package version.
- Run `uv run knowledge-tracker config` and confirm the output shows the default data directory, log level, limit, and package version.
- Run `KNOWLEDGE_TRACKER_LOG_LEVEL=DEBUG uv run knowledge-tracker config` and verify the printed log level changes to `DEBUG`.
- Because `--log-level` is a global flag on the main parser, place it before the subcommand. Run `uv run knowledge-tracker --log-level ERROR config` and verify the CLI flag overrides the environment variable, displaying `ERROR` instead.

Next Steps

Recap of skills gained

You now have a solid foundation in Python 3.14. You can install and manage interpreters with `uv`, structure packages with `pyproject.toml`, and write typed, tested functions using deferred annotations and template strings. You have built a working CLI application that uses classes, protocols, and custom exceptions; handles file I/O and async boundaries; and runs through a full CI-ready toolchain including `pytest`, `mypy`, and `ruff`. You have also seen how free-threaded Python and subinterpreters change the concurrency landscape, giving you a practical base for future architecture decisions.

Recommended next projects

Apply what you have learned by building something self-contained. Try a URL bookmark manager with async metadata fetching, a local JSON API using the standard library `http.server` and `socketserver`, or a batch file renamer that reads configuration from TOML. Pick a project that forces you to write unit tests, add type hints, and manage dependencies with `uv`. Revisit the tracker from this book and extend it: add a SQLite backend, a `curses` TUI, or a WebSocket feed. Teaching someone else how to use `uv init` or `pytest` will reinforce your own fluency.

Suggested advanced topics to learn next

Move deeper into static typing by studying generics, `TypeVar`, and `TypedDict`. Explore CPython internals by reading the `ceval.c` or the `ast` module documentation. If concurrency interests you, profile free-threaded workloads and experiment with `concurrent.interpreters` in larger scripts. For web development, study ASGI and `httpx`. For systems programming, look at `ctypes`, `cffi`, or Rust extensions with `PyO3` and `maturin`. Each path builds on the typing, testing, and packaging habits you formed here.

How to stay current

Read the official documentation at docs.python.org and the "What's New" pages for each release. Follow PEP discussions on peps.python.org to understand features before they land. Monitor changelogs for `uv`, `ruff`, `pytest`, and `mypy` to keep your toolchain sharp. Join the Python Discourse, attend local meetups, and watch PyCon talks. The language and its ecosystem evolve quickly; regular reading and small experiments will keep your skills relevant and your projects maintainable.

Part V: Review Questions

Answer Key

Chapter 1: Hello, Python 3.14

1. D
2. D
3. D
4. A
5. C
6. A

Chapter 2: Values, Expressions, Strings, and Types

1. D
2. A
3. C
4. C
5. D

Chapter 3: Control Flow and CLI Routing

1. A
2. D
3. C
4. A
5. C
6. D

Chapter 4: Functions, Scope, and Deferred Annotations

1. C

2. D
3. A
4. D
5. C

Chapter 5: Collections, Iteration, and Comprehensions

1. A
2. D
3. A
4. B
5. B

Chapter 6: Files, Paths, I/O, and Basic File Errors

1. B
2. C
3. B
4. C
5. B

Chapter 7: Modules, Packages, and Project Layout

1. B
2. B
3. B
4. C
5. B

Chapter 8: Classes, Dataclasses, and Protocols

1. B

2. C
3. A
4. C
5. B

Chapter 9: Application Errors, Exceptions, and Logging

1. C
2. C
3. B
4. A
5. A

Chapter 10: Async I/O and Concurrency Choices

1. C
2. C
3. B
4. B
5. C

Chapter 11: Testing and Type Checking

1. B
2. B
3. C
4. B
5. A
6. B

Chapter 12: Toolchain, Configuration, Performance, and Deployment

1. B
2. C
3. B
4. C
5. B

Thank You for Reading

We hope this book has been a valuable resource in your learning journey.

Join the unQbd Community

You just built a typed, tested Python 3.14 CLI application using uv, pytest, and mypy. Now imagine pushing that same rigor into free-threaded concurrency, advanced generics, and systems programming with the rest of the unQbd library.

Visit unqbd.com/app to start your 7-day Premium trial, then $9.99 per year.

Every book. Every audiobook. $9.99 for the entire year.

Prefer to explore first?

Create a free account at **unqbd.com/register/free** to access curated books, community reviews, and weekly free releases.

If this book helped you, a quick review on Amazon helps other readers find it. Thank you.

www.ingramcontent.com/pod-product-compliance
Lightning Source LLC
LaVergne TN
LVHW060033210926
848481LV00013B/3846

Praise for Earth Sanctuary's Sacred Ecology

Earth Sanctuary is a combination of wilderness and a magnificent lovingly crafted garden. It's like an enchanted forest.

Meditating together in the stone circle and in the dolmen. Sitting by the Fen Pond, watching the beaver and ducks while the sun was setting. I don't know when I've felt so full of peace. Sharing that with my son has been priceless.

Each Walk into the sanctuary brought new wonders...the first day I ran across deer twice and watched a piliated woodpecker for a long time. The second day I saw three deer and had a long conversation with a small bird, then watched a Great Blue Heron take flight. The sacred sites yielded profound meditative experiences, especially the Prayer Stone and the Medicine Wheels...it is lovely how you've posted protocols for use to make them accessible.

One of the most healing places I have ever been. The Earth here is truly healing – it is the process of healing, and it is healing for us. Spectacular. Thank you!

Thank you for all that you've done to create the magical, serene, and most exceptional spiritual space here at the Earth's Sanctuary...that's truly what it is. I couldn't be more grateful. An experience of a lifetime!

What Chuck and His team are doing here is amazing. 'It is better to light one small candle than to curse the darkness.' Many well-meaning people are cursing activities that degrade earth and threaten many species. Chuck is doing a great job of lighting a candle.

How special and important to be in a forest that exists for the sake of the forest, itself.

I didn't know what to expect. This place is overwhelming, all the beauty, the solitude. I had quite an experience in the Fen stone circle, one I will never forget. I can't wait to come back.

What a beautiful marriage of ecological restoration and spiritual renewal! Special in every way – a sensory ecological delight.

This is a Sanctuary for life and for finding life within yourself. Release your sufferings to Mother Earth and be Renewed.

"This sanctuary is one of the most grounding, loving spaces that was perfect for my mom and I. Thank you for creating such a sacred, welcoming space.

The energy here is amazing. As soon as I arrived, I felt a sense of calm and my anxiety faded away. While we were out on the trail, we observed an owl in one of the trees. This was my first sighting ever of an owl in the wild. We observed the osprey while hiking around the Middle Path trail which was the first encounter of an osprey sighting for both of us. Your trails are well kept and easy to follow without getting lost. I heard the humming of the universe near the Fen Pond. I haven't been able to hear this before during contemplation and meditation. It's truly remarkable how the ley lines make such a difference in the energy vibrating in certain areas. Thank you for sharing your beautiful, magical place with us!

We found the energy in the Fen Stone Circle to be very powerful. We are in appreciation of the dedication that has been gifted to this place. It is very evident that the earth here is holding the loving energy for all that visit and for all mankind.

What I liked best about Earth Sanctuary was the peaceful, quiet natural setting and being able to have quiet alone time, with myself and our wildlife neighbors.

There is a beating heart of love at the center of the universe. Thank you for this place of beauty and healing that allowed me to hear it.

We are deeply grateful to enjoy this beautiful space. The experience was very healing for our family.

A blessed place to process, meditate, renew the spirit. A powerful place with magical energy.

A powerful reminder that all places are sacred and that we sometimes notice it. Earth Sanctuary shares the invitation with spaces of many traditions, so one is likely to find a place somewhere that resonates. Encountering a stone ring unexpectedly in the dusk took my sense by surprise. How do you put words on the unspeakable? It happened. Thank you. Your ways of doing this inspire me.

While doing some quiet chanting yesterday in the Earth Sanctuary's spectacular Dolmen, a hummingbird came into the space and hovered for a long time like a blessings to my meditation. What an incredible sanctuary this is that even the birds feel safe and happy to join in the space.!

"The fen and bog island are pure magic. The grounds at Earth Sanctuary are so thoughtfully designed to provide solitude and peace to the spiritual visitor."